CIVILIZATION ONE

Previous books by Christopher Knight
(co–authored with Robert Lomas)

The Hiram Key
The Second Messiah
Uriel's machine
The Book of Hiram

Previous books by Alan Butler
The Bronze Age Computer Disc
 The Warriors and the Bankers
The Templar Continuum
 The Goddess, the Grail and the Lodge

Christopher Knight has worked in advertising and marketing for over thirty years, specializing in consumer psychology and market research.

His writing career began almost by accident after he had invested seven years conducting research into the origins of Freemasonic rituals and he has written four books to date, co-authored with Robert Lomas. His first book, *The Hiram Key* was published in 1996 and it immediately went into the UK top ten, best-seller list and remained in the chart for eight consecutive weeks. It has since been translated into 37 languages and sold over a million copies worldwide, becoming a best seller in several countries. He now divides his time between marketing consultancy and historical research for writing books.

Alan Butler qualified as an engineer, but was always fascinated by history, and made himself into something of an expert in astrology and astronomy. Since 1990, he has been researching ancient cultures, pagan beliefs and comparative religion and has published four successful books on such topics as the Knights Templar and the Grail legend. He is also a published playwright and a very successful radio dramatist.

CIVILIZATION ONE

THE WORLD IS NOT AS YOU THOUGHT IT WAS

Christopher Knight and Alan Butler

WATKINS PUBLISHING
LONDON

This edition published in the UK 2004 by
Watkins Publishing, Sixth Floor, Castle House,
75-76 Wells Street, London W1T 3QH

Designed and typeset by Jerry Goldie
Printed and bound in Great Britain

British Library Cataloguing in Publication data available
Library of Congress Cataloging in Publication data available

ISBN 1 84293 095 8

www.watkinspublishing.com
www.civilizationone.com

Contents

Introduction

PLATES

The Ring of Brodgar, Orkney, Scotland
Stonehenge on Salisbury Plain, England
The observatory at Newgrange, Ireland
A clay pendulum
A Megalithic bowl
A cube of water
A cube of barley
A pint cube in clay
The statue of King Gudea, ruler of the city state, Lagash
    (c 2050–2000 BC)
A barley cubit
A barley inch
Modern measurement of a barley seed
The ruins of the Minoan Palace of Knossos, Crete
Thomas Jefferson (1743–1826)
Jefferson's rod
The Phaistos Disc
The Earth
The Moon
The Sun
A solar eclipse
The planet Venus
Chart of the Relationship between Music and Visible Light

DEDICATIONS

For my grandchildren Sam, Isabelle and Max (plus others
yet to arrive). May your childhood wonder and questioning
stay with you for life.

CK

For my Father, John Butler, and in memory of my Mother Mary.

AB

A CD of Megalithic music has been composed and performed by
De Lorean to accompany this book. Samples of *Civilization One –
The Album* can be heard and copies bought at
www.civilizationone.com.

Acknowledgements

Kate Butler, for her invaluable help with the index.

Fred Cameron, for his important comments regarding the Sumerians.

Fiona Spencer-Thomas, for efforts above and beyond the call of duty.

Michael Mann, whose close cooperation and advice was essential to this book.

Penny Stopa and the Editorial team.

Tony Crerar, for his welcome contributions.

Hilary Newbigin, for her most welcome advice.

Peter Harwood, our technical expert.

Introduction

The super-culture

Was there a super-advanced culture in prehistory? If not, how can it be that the supposedly unsophisticated people of Stone Age Britain possessed a fully-integrated system of measurement based on a deep understanding of the solar system?

The history of human development from hunter-gatherer to city dwellers once seemed comfortable and predictable. All of the available evidence supported the accepted picture of a smooth social evolution largely driven by the ingenuity of people living in the Middle East. But then, over several decades, an eminent professor of engineering, Alexander Thom, annoyed the world of archaeology by making a startling claim. He maintained that he had found that the structures left by late Stone Age man had been built using a standard unit of measure that was so precise that he could identify its central value to an accuracy that was less than the width of a human hair. The idea that these simple people from prehistory could have achieved such accuracy flew in the face of all the worldview of most archaeologists. Not surprisingly, Thom's findings were almost universally dismissed as some kind of mistake.

Professor Thom called his discovered unit the 'Megalithic Yard', but he died (in 1985) without ever being able to explain why people from the Neolithic Period, or late Stone Age, circa 3500 BC might have been motivated to establish such a measure or how they could have consistently reproduced such incredible accuracy.

Even today there are many tens of thousands of these Megalithic stone structures strewn across the British Isles and the western fringes of Europe. Our initial quest was simple: we wanted to find out if Thom really had found a prehistoric measure or if he had been deluded by the huge amount of data he collected from his surveying of sites from the islands of northern Scotland down to Brittany on the west coast of France. We reasoned that if Thom's Megalithic Yard was imaginary, it should be a meaningless value, but if it was indeed a genuine Neolithic measure, it should have some physical reality behind it and some kind of scientific means of reproduction.

The consequences of knowledge

Our investigation led us to a rediscovery of the science behind this prehistoric unit: we can now demonstrate both its mathematical origin and its means of reproduction, using the mass and spin of the Earth. In identifying the precise origin of Thom's Megalithic Yard, however, we soon found that we had nudged open the door of a virtual treasure chest of lost knowledge.

Our approach has been to apply forensic techniques to archaeology across a span of cultures from prehistory (before 3000 BC) and the earliest times of written history (after 3000 BC). We have found that there is a completely identifiable 'DNA' associated with the oldest and purest system of science that appears in the most unexpected places. Even units of measure that are believed to be relatively modern, from the pound and the pint to the gram and the litre, turn out to be thousands of years old and linked to the very dimensions of the solar system.

We have tried to keep our story as short and as clear as possible. A basic knowledge of arithmetic is all that is required to follow our investigation in detail, so please have your calculator to hand if you wish to check our findings step by step. Additional information, frequently asked questions and new developments are available on our website: www.civilizationone.com.

If you feel comfortable with the old idea that human development was a smooth evolutionary journey from ignorant caveman to urban sophisticate, be prepared to be shocked. The world is not what you thought it was.

CHAPTER 1

The Great Wall of History

The invention of writing

Forget the wheel – it was the invention of writing that changed our world forever.

The first wheels were used for turning clay pots and were later attached to axles to improve the efficiency of moving across dry ground for agriculture and warfare. This certainly helped in the production of food and aided its distribution to the growing communities that became the earliest cities, but major movements of people and goods relied mainly on sea lanes and inland waterways for thousands of years. The use of writing, however, had an immediate effect on commerce. Some of the earliest documents created were concerned with ships' manifests and other documents of trade. Lunar calendars existed from as early as 20,000 BC, carved on bone or antler, but 'real' writing developed extremely quickly in Sumer and Egypt circa 3000 BC. It was this ability to record information without relying on the honesty and memory of others that really drove mankind forward to begin an age that we define as the beginning of civilization, circa 3200 BC.

The first great breakthrough in communication had happened nearly two million years earlier when our distant ancestors, *Homo erectus*, developed a larynx position lower in the throat than other primates. This piece of evolution cost these creatures their ability to breathe and drink at the same time, but it allowed them to generate a far wider range of sounds than had previously been possible. With a vocabulary of thousands of discernible sounds, spoken language is thought to have developed very quickly.

The simplest form of vocal communication may have been a hunting ploy, for example to imitate the sound of an animal and then point to its direction. Over time true language developed as abstract sounds were used to represent objects and actions and then assembled into sentences to express complex issues such as human emotions. Language allowed for information to be passed on from one person to another but the next stage of development was to make a record of human knowledge and experience by drawing a representation of the subject matter. We can see that the drawings on the walls of prehistoric caves are a kind of proto-writing. Any mark that records a specific meaning, either to the originator or to others, can fairly be called basic writing. The first writing systems were made up of hieroglyphs, which were used like a cartoon strip of pictures to contain information. These early writing methods came into use just over 5,000 years ago and slowly developed into abstract notation where the marks have a meaning that can only be understood by those people trained in the process of encodement and decodement – reading. But it seems that sophisticated meaning has been communicated by 'writing' for a great deal longer than has been thought.

Dr Michael Rappenglueck of the University of Munich has shown how a 16,000-year-old drawing of a horse in the caves at Lascaux in France is actually a carefully recorded lunar calendar.[1] What, at first view, looks like a very attractive drawing of horse, is now thought to be a means of keeping track of the phases of the Moon. This surely qualifies as writing.

This level of intelligence in Palaeolithic Man is hardly surprising. As a species, *Homo sapiens* has not changed significantly either mentally or physically, for well over 100,000 years. We may have moved from the Stone Age to the Internet Age but each human being is no different today to their forebear 500 generations in the past. We must also remember that while most of us have lives that have been shaped by the technological revolution, there are some groups of people around the world who still live as simple hunter-gatherers in a genuinely Stone Age existence, for example some Australian Aborigines and tribes in some parts of South America.

The remarkable Sumerians

Given that speech has been around for so long, it would be surprising if communication through drawn symbols only arrived so very recently. The earliest form of writing that is generally accepted as such emerged more or less at the same time as the wheel. Both were invented by the remarkable Sumarian people, who arrived in the land now known as Iraq from an unknown location more than 5,000 years ago. The Egyptians devised their earliest hieroglyphic system very shortly afterwards (probably within 200 years), just when Upper and Lower Egypt were united into a single kingdom.

The so-called cuneiform (from the Latin *cuneus* meaning 'wedge') characters developed by the Sumerians were made by pressing wedge-shaped sticks into wet clay. These Sumerian tablets may look rather unimpressive to us today but these 'talking' patterns were thought to

[1] http://news.bbc.co.uk/1/hi/sci/tech/975360.stm

have powerful magic by ordinary people. At first, the content of these documents was very basic, but as time went by improvements added layers of sophistication until around 800 BC when the Greeks created a full alphabetic writing system that finally separated consonants from vowels. The period immediately before these early records were left by the Sumerians and the Ancient Egyptians has become a virtual wall, separating what we call 'history' from everything that happened before – which we label 'pre-history'. Everything that occurred before the advent of true writing is now considered to be myth and legend because every piece of human knowledge had to be transmitted by word of mouth from generation to generation.

The Great Wall of History

This 'wall' effect actually says a great deal more about current thinking than it does about the people who occupied our world before history began. Being human, we tend to view ourselves, and our society, as being somehow definitive – the measure of 'rightness' by which to gauge others. During the 19th and the first half of the 20th centuries, there was an egocentric worldview in academia whereby white, Christian, male explorers would travel to see the 'inferior' races who did not live 'properly'. One English naturalist wrote of his disdain for a group in Tierra del Fuego who shouted at him from a canoe:

> 'Viewing such men, one can hardly make oneself believe that they are fellow creatures, and inhabitants of the same world. We often try to imagine what pleasures in life some of the lower animals can enjoy: how much more reasonably the same questions may be asked concerning these barbarians.'

These were the words of the young Charles Darwin, a man who went on to realize how all humanity has sprung from lower animals.

8

Today, academia is much more objective and less judgemental than in previous generations, but the ideal of anything approaching real empathy is frequently as distant as it ever was for much of archaeology. But, we would argue, if we really want to bring into finer focus the landscape that lies beyond the Great Wall of History, we must undergo something of a fundamental shift in our mind-set.

The subject matter of this book requires readers to open their minds to a softer, more yielding worldview that dissolves preconceptions and temporarily allows the mind to roam freely over the subject matter, thereby allowing consideration of possibilities that might otherwise be missed. The principle that appears to underpin standard academia these days can reasonably be called 'stepping stone' logic, where deductions are often only encouraged in a strictly linear fashion. By this mode of reasoning one can only proceed by confirming each step before looking for an incremental way forward. While it sounds entirely sensible, it can blind the researcher to factors that are outside their expectations. Albert Einstein is famously said to have observed that 'Imagination is more important than knowledge'. Surely the great man has to be right: true insights come from thinking outside the box rather than simply ticking procedural boxes in a neat row.

A very famous archaeologist once said to Alan that all of his findings must be dismissed because his starting point was, in his opinion, wrong. How foolish. Even if someone does start with an error it is entirely possible that subsequent discoveries could be right if validated without reliance on the original premise.

The mode of reasoning that we invite you, the reader, to adopt while reading this book is one we call the 'tepee method'. This is a multi-dimensional approach to logical deduction rather than a classical linear 'stepping stone' process. It simply requires that each piece of evidence is seen in its own right and is not forced to conform to any preconceived notion of what *should* be. Even where different elements of evidence appear to be mutually exclusive, we suggest that they should be allowed to coexist until the time comes for a final analysis. With the tepee method each strand of evidence is considered to be a potential supporting stick – and only if there are eventually enough of them that work together does the argument stand. We believe that this is the only approach to examining the distant past that is likely to produce a cogent picture, one that does not pick and choose which facts it prefers to accept as 'real'. As we conducted our research there were many occasions where we felt the urge to reject a finding as a coincidence because it did not fit with what we expected to see. We suspended our judgement and eventually, as a new picture emerged, we were very glad that we had not tried to force our preconceptions on the evidence.

Any readers who feel unable to open their minds right up at this point should close the book now.

The Ancient Egyptians

The Great Wall of History has distorted the way most people view the past by telescoping events so that the Ancient Egyptian civilization is often thought of as being extremely distant, whereas in terms of the span of the existence of our fully-developed species, it was actually extremely recent.

The huge array of artefacts and records left by the Ancient Egyptians provides a wonderfully strong picture of their lives and achievements. We know the names of kings right back to King Menes who unified the two lands of Upper and Lower Egypt in approximately 3100 BC and ruled from the capital of Memphis at the head of the Nile Delta. This great civilization left us beautiful structures such as the Giza pyramids and the Sphinx – and we can even medically examine the physical remains of Egypt's rulers and leading citizens, carefully preserved by skilful mummification. Archaeologists have estimated that the Egyptians embalmed huge numbers of bodies. Though seeming to be a massive number, some claim that as many as 730 million people may have been mummified between the time of King Menes and the 7th century AD, when the practice was ended.[2] Although many mummies have not survived the scorching heat of northern Africa, it is believed that several million are preserved in yet-to-be-discovered tombs and burial places. As recently as June 1999 a burial ground containing almost 10,000 mummies was discovered near the town of Bawiti, southwest of Cairo.

We know what these people ate, with whom they traded, as well as when and against whom they went to war. One 5,000-year-old Egyptian mace head contains a record of a great victory in which no less than 120,000 prisoners were taken, together with 400,000 oxen and 1,422,000 goats that were liberated from the enemy.[3] King Khufu, who built the Great Pyramid, was even kind enough to leave us a dismantled boat that has now been rebuilt. As a result, we can be sure that the Egyptians used only wood, rope, reeds and the like for their craft, which contained no metal.

These people also left detailed records of their gods and their religious practices. The famous Book of the Dead is a large collection of funerary texts from various dates, containing magical formulae, hymns, and prayers believed by the ancient Egyptians to guide and protect the soul of the deceased on its journey into the land of the dead. The texts tell us of a belief that happiness in the afterlife was dependent on having led a life in keeping with a principle known as 'Maat' – which meant doing good to all others.

[2] http://nabataea.net/items.html
[3] http://www.math.buffalo.edu/mad/Ancient-Africa/mad_ancient_egypt.html

The dark side of the Wall

These examples make the point that our knowledge of the Ancient Egyptian people on this side of the Great Wall of History is very extensive – but we know only very limited amounts of what happened on the dark side of the wall. For example, the Greek historian Herodotus, referred to as the 'father of history' for his nine-volume work written in the early 5th century BC, observed of Egypt that 'there is no country that possesses so many wonders, nor any that has such a number of works which defy description'. Herodotus is considered to be the starting point of Western historical writing, although the accuracy of his facts has often been doubted by modern scholars because they seemed to be laden with exaggeration. However, archaeological finds have begun to show that this Greek chronicler was extremely accurate. For example, Herodotus had described the great city wall of Babylon as having buildings placed on top of it and yet still having 'enough space between for a four-horse chariot to turn'. This seemed unlikely to experts but remains have been discovered indicating that the wall was of such a width.

Thanks to early scribes and historians like Herodotus we have a rich knowledge of the last 5,000 years, but what do we know of cultures that blossomed before this time?

After 100,000 years of what is assumed to be virtual stagnation, humans began a completely new way of life in what is known as the Neolithic Revolution. It began approximately 12,000 years ago when people across the Middle East, Europe and Asia quite suddenly abandoned their nomadic hunter-gatherer existence and began to opt for permanent settlements. They began to cultivate rice, wheat, rye, peas, lentils and other plants, and to domesticate animals such as cattle, sheep, pigs, and goats. Technology also began around this time with the manufacture of pottery vessels for cooking and storing food, stone sickles, and grinding stones to turn grain into flour.

The term 'Neolithic' means new Stone Age, and it refers to the time when the first farmers tilled the soil, planted, watered and harvested their crops and cared for their newly-domesticated animals all the year round. In the British Isles the Neolithic Period can be said to span from approximately 6000–1500 BC. This new lifestyle was more labour-intensive than hunting and gathering but also more certain, and it may be the case that the Neolithic Revolution was caused by the need to produce more food as a result of an increase in population. According to standard interpretations of the available evidence, the world had created the platform upon which civilization would eventually be built, but from our perspective these early farmers were still very crude and unsophisticated because they existed on the dark side of the Great Wall of History. However, there was one Stone Age culture that appears to dramatically upset such a neat paradigm.

Builders and artists

On the western fringes of Europe there was a culture that left tens of thousands of structures that still stand today. From parts of Scandinavia and the Baltic, down to northern Spain and especially throughout the British Isles these long-departed people built with enormous stones and are therefore remembered as the Megalithic builders – a name that literally means 'giant stones'. The terms 'Neolithic' and 'Megalithic' tend to be used interchangeably because it was these new Stone Age people who built the giant stone monuments. In the fifth and fourth millennia BC these supposedly primitive builders created huge circles and other structures using stones weighing up to 350 tonnes, such as the 20-metre-high 'Le Grand Menhir Brisée' in Brittany. On the banks of the River Boyne in Ireland they left a beautiful circular construction now known as Newgrange, a massive structure and 1,000 years older than the Great Pyramid in Egypt. But these people left very little else to tell us about their lives and beliefs. They had no writing as such, while most of their artefacts that were not stone or pottery have long since rotted to nothing in the damp European climate.

Particular and highly important members of the Megalithic builders have been named after the pottery fragments found around their encampments. They are sometimes simply called the 'Grooved Ware People' on account of the grooved patterns they chose to etch into the wet clay of their cooking utensils.

For thousands of years the massive stone structures these people so painstakingly created stood in silence. They were known as 'fairy mounds' by rural folk or sometimes uprooted by more pragmatic farmers to clear the land or to use the stone for their own building requirements. Few people gave any thought to the age or purpose of these giants in stone, until archaeology evolved as a serious discipline in the late 1800s. Even then, most early archaeologists were more interested in the exciting potential offered by excavations in places such as Egypt and Mesopotamia than in the British Isles and Europe.

The heavenly architects

It is now known that these mysterious people from the other side of the Great Wall of History had a significant interest in astronomy, and many of the larger Megalithic sites have been shown to have solar, lunar and stellar alignments. From the Ring of Brodgar in Orkney in the far north of Scotland, to Stonehenge in southern England and to the stone rows of Brittany in France, specialists have come to recognize that these people spent a lot of time observing the movements of the heavens. Newgrange in Ireland, for example, has a single shaft that was carefully constructed to allow the light of Venus to penetrate a central chamber once every eight years on the winter solstice, shortly before dawn.[4]

Venus moves in such a way that it has a predictable 40-year cycle, made up of five patterns of eight years, giving the engineers who designed and built the Newgrange observatory a calendar so accurate that it can only be beaten today by the use of atomic clocks.

Alexander Thom and Archaeoastronomy

So, it is possible to understand something of the abilities and interests of the Neolithic culture, even without the benefit of writing. One man above all others was the pioneer of a discipline that is now known as 'archaeoastronomy' – his name was Alexander Thom.

Alexander Thom was born in Scotland in 1894. He became a student at Glasgow University and later returned as a lecturer in engineering. During the Second World War he worked for the British government but in 1945 he moved to Oxford University, where he became Professor of Engineering, a post he held until his retirement in 1961. His investigations into Megalithic sites spanned 50 years and did not end until very close to his death in 1985.

Thom's interest in Megalithic structures began in his native Scotland, where he noticed that such sites appeared to have lunar alignments. In the early 1930s he decided to study some of the sites and began a process of careful surveying that was to take him almost five decades. In addition to his lecturing, Alexander Thom was a highly-talented engineer in his own right and he taught himself surveying, which enabled him to look at more Megalithic sites – and in greater detail – than anyone before or since.

From his first survey at Callanish, in the Hebrides off the west coast of Scotland, Thom realized that far from being crudely erected these structures had been carefully designed. He began to appreciate that the

---

[4] Knight, C. and Lomas, R.: *Uriel's Machine*. Arrow, London, 2000.

prehistoric engineers had an advanced knowledge of geometry and astronomy and must have been highly-skilled surveyors.

Thom continued his careful surveying before publishing an article in 1951 in the *Journal of the British Astronomical Association* entitled 'The solar observations of megalithic man'. The results of his careful measuring of Megalithic sites were also published in three articles over several years in the *Journal of the Royal Statistical Society*, the first appearing in 1955 and also in his three books.

The approach taken by Professor Thom was entirely different to that adopted by any archaeologist. Looking at the scale and obvious planning involved in Megalithic sites, Thom had been forced to conclude that the planners and builders must have been very able engineers – just like himself. He knew that their level of knowledge was far below his own but he had no reason to doubt their intellectual ability and ingenuity. He therefore carefully analyzed what remained of each site and then tried to imagine what it was that the builders had set out to achieve. Once he had a picture in his mind of what he thought their plan had been, he went away to create his own solution to the assumed problem. Having drawn up his own design he then returned to compare the site layout to his own blueprint.

Mind-set and vision

This simple yet radical approach was a stroke of genius. Thom quickly developed a total empathy with the Megalithic builders. After all, who else can better understand the mind-set of an engineer than another engineer? Here was a leading academic who had changed his thinking to look at the other side of the Great Wall of History. Thom did not assume anything about the Megalithic builders other than to acknowledge that they must have been skilled engineers. Unlike the archaeologists of the day he was not searching for more clues to confirm existing theories and he had gathered data for many years before he even attempted to make sense of it.

Thom developed an understanding of the Megalithic mind and found that he could predict the location of missing stones; on further inspection, he would usually reveal the socket hole that confirmed his expectation. This engineer had a view of the landscape beyond the Great Wall of History that was denied to standard archaeologists who were limiting themselves to increasing numbers of similar excavations. Reassembling broken pots and analyzing discarded food items in rubbish heaps can indeed be very revealing about the realities of day-to-day life in the Neolithic Period, but it tells us virtually nothing about the aspirations of the builders and sheer enthusiasm for knowledge that appear to have emanated from the souls of these people.

The Megalithic Yard

Thom made detailed studies of every site he explored and developed a new statistical technique to establish the relative positions of the stones. Slowly, something totally unexpected emerged from the amassed data. It appeared that the vast majority of these prehistoric sites, from the islands off northern Scotland down to the coast of Brittany, had been constructed using a standard unit of measurement. According to Thom, the units he discovered were extraordinary because they were scientifically exact. Virtually all known units of measurement from the Sumerians and Ancient Egyptians through to the Middle Ages are believed to have been based on average body parts such as fingers, hands, feet and arms, and were therefore quite approximate. Thom identified a unit that had been used in an area that stretched from northern Scotland to western France, and appears in Neolithic structures built during the 4th–2nd millennia BC. His definition of this unit of length was that it was equal to

2.722 feet/82.966 centimetres.[5] He named this unit a 'Megalithic Yard' because it was only a few inches less than a standard yard. He found that this Megalithic Yard had been used in multiples, including half and double forms as well as being divided into 40 sub-units that he called 'Megalithic Inches'.

In 1955, after analysing the data from the surveying of 46 circular stone rings, Thom concluded that they had been laid out as multiples of a standard unit of measurement that had been used throughout Britain.[6] Alexander Thom and his son Archie, who had begun to assist him in his work, eventually arrived at a definitive length for the Megalithic Yard of 2.722 feet +/− 0.002 feet (82.96656cm +/− 0.061cm).[7]

Thom found small variations in the length of his Megalithic Yard but the distribution of error was utterly consistent, centring on a tiny range − not a fuzzy zone as would be expected from an ancient measure. The distribution graph of variations kept powerfully centring on a single point.

The engineer was utterly perplexed, since he could not begin to explain his own findings. He was well aware that even if there had been a priesthood that cut poles to the required length and then passed them on over the tens of thousands of square miles involved and across many generations, such uncanny accuracy could not have been the result. In 1968 he wrote:

'This unit was in use from one end of Britain to the other. It is not possible to detect by statistical examination any differences between the values determined in the English and Scottish circles.

---

[5] Thom, A.: *Megalithic Sites in Britain*. Clarendon Press, London, 1967.
[6] Thom A.: 'A statistical examination of the Megalithic sites in Britain'. (1955) *Journal of the Royal Statistical Society*, A118, 275-91.
[7] Thom and Thom: *Megalithic Remains in Britain and Brittany*. Oxford University Press, Oxford, 1978. Chapters 3,4, 6, 7 & 8.

There must have been a headquarters from which standard rods [a rod could be of two types, but in this context they are pieces of wood cut to represent the Megalithic Yard] were sent out... The length of rods in Scotland cannot have differed from that in England by more than 0.03 inch [*0.762 mm*] or the difference would have shown up. If each small community had obtained the length by copying the rod from its neighbour to the south the accumulated error would have been much greater than this.' [8]

At that time Thom's data could not be explained by any mechanism known to be available to the people of the late Stone Age other than to assume that all rods were made at the same place and delivered by hand to each and every community across Scotland and England. Eventually he would find the unit in use from the Hebrides to western France, which makes the central ruler factory theory look most unlikely. He also found it impossible to imagine why these early communities wanted to work to an exact standard unit.

Although he could not explain it, Thom stood by his data. While he was puzzled, many people within the archaeological community were not. For most archaeologists it was a simple case of an engineer playing with something he did not understand and getting his facts wrong. This was not an unreasonable response because the culture that produced the Megalithic structures had left no other signs of such sophistication. Thom's data was accepted but its interpretation was almost universally rejected. However, when the Royal Society under the auspices of Professor Kendal was asked to check his work in order to find the error, it responded by stating that there was one chance in a hundred that Thom's Megalithic Yard had *not* been employed on the sites surveyed.

[8] Thom, A.: *Megalithic Sites in Britain*. Oxford University Press, Oxford, 1968.

Despite the fact that a number of leading archaeologists has subsequently identified accumulations close to whole number (integer) multiples of a unit of approximately 0.83 metres.[9] Thom's work is still largely ignored on the basis that it is wholly inconsistent with scholarly opinion of the abilities of Neolithic Man. A failure to explain how this culture could have achieved such an accurate system of measurement has caused the archaeological community to disbelieve Thom's findings and put them down as some kind of statistical blunder. A suggestion was put forward that Thom's extensive data might reveal nothing more than the average pace or footstep of all the people involved in the building of these structures. After all, if enough data is collected and examined it is bound to produce an average, assuming that people paced out large distances and used their palm-widths for smaller ones. At first this explanation sounds very reasonable, even probable. But Professor Thom was not a fool – and he would have been a very poor mathematician to make such a basic mistake. The reality is that the 'human pace' theory is not a possible solution to the finding of a standard unit for two reasons. First, because the human stride varies far more than the small deviations found and second, because the distribution curve would be an entirely different shape. This 'solution' to the data is simply wrong.

The difference in approach between Thom and the general archaeological community is fundamental. In simple terms, archaeologists are experts in the recovery and cataloguing of manufactured artefacts that allows them to understand rates of development and influences between groups. They dig up the remains of human settlements and

[9] Heggie, D. C.: *Megalithic Science: Ancient Mathematics and Astronomy in Northwest Europe*. Thames and Hudson, London, 1981. *See also*: Renfrew, C. & Bahn, P. G.: *Archaeology: Theory, Methods and Practice, Second Edition*. Thames and Hudson, London, 1996.

piece together some idea of the community involved from written records and from lost or discarded items. This process works well in places such as Egypt where there is an almost boundless supply of artefacts and documents to give us an insight into the lives of its people. However, the procedure is less than satisfactory when considering the structures of Megalithic Europe because there are few artefacts to be retrieved and no written records at all.

Dr Aubrey Burl, the highly respected archaeologist whom Thom quoted extensively, confirmed to us that he did not believe in the reality of the Megalithic Yard, stating that he had excavated many Megalithic sites but had never found the measurement. This statement reveals a collision of techniques since it is difficult to itemize one specific Megalithic Yard at any ancient site. This is because the unit in the sense Thom often found it only reveals itself from the careful gathering of huge amounts of data extracted from every site.

Although individual standing stones have been shown by Thom to have moved very little over the centuries, an entire site must be meticulously catalogued before the Megalithic Yard really makes its presence felt.

Douglas Heggie of Edinburgh University gives the arguments against the validity of the results claimed by Thom in their most complete form in a book, where he questions the validity of the statistical approach.[10] Heggie suggested that having 'found' what he thought was the Megalithic Yard, Professor Thom, particularly in his later work, might have had his findings coloured by the expectation of certain results. He also questioned how Thom had decided on the point on any given stone in any structure from which to take his measurements. From his own approach to assessing Thom's work Heggie came to the conclusion that if the Megalithic Yard existed at all it probably only did so in Scotland, and even then to a much less accurate degree of tolerance than Professor Thom had claimed.

Douglas Heggie is a highly respected professor of mathematics and Alexander Thom was a highly respected professor of engineering – so who is right? Most archaeologists prefer to side with Heggie, almost certainly because the whole idea of a prehistoric unit of measurement is at odds with their view of Neolithic achievements. But archaeologists who have carefully reviewed Thom's work in the field have a different view. For example, Tony Crerar, a researcher and engineer in Wales and Euan Mackie, an honorary Research Fellow at the Hunterian Institute in Scotland are strong supporters of the concept of the Megalithic Yard. Dr Mackie has recently said of Thom:

> 'By exact surveying and statistical analysis he (Thom) demon-strated that most stone circles could have been set out much more accurately than previously supposed. Most are truly circular with diameters set out in units of a 'megalithic yard' of 0.829 metres or 2.72 feet. Other circles had more complex shapes like ellipses and flattened circles, whose dimensions appear to be based on pythagorean triangles, also measured in megalithic yards. By similar means he showed that many standing stone sites pointed at notches and mountain peaks on the horizon where the Sun or Moon rose or set at significant times. Not only does a sophisticated solar calendar seem to have been in use, but the Moon's movements may have been studied carefully, even up to the level of eclipse prediction.' [11]

There were question marks over the Megalithic Yard but the challenge laid down by the late Professor Alexander Thom still remained.

[10] Heggie, D. C.: *Megalithic Science: Ancient Mathematics and Astronomy in Northwest Europe*. Thames and Hudson, London, 1981.
[11] Mackie, E. W.: July 30th 2003, see: http://www.dealbhadair.co.uk/athom.htm

In our opinion there were only two main possibilities:

1. Thom's data gathering and/or his analysis were flawed, and the Megalithic builders did not use the Megalithic Yard as a standard system of measurement.
2. Thom's data and his analysis were both correct. The Megalithic builders did use this standard unit of measurement and it was applied with great accuracy.

'Stick to Facts, sir!'

It is a matter of record that the academic establishment prefers a gentle evolution to revolution in its thinking. No academic authority enjoys having its finely-tuned paradigm challenged. But it is time to put the Megalithic Yard to the test. So, was there a way forward to resolve the authenticity or otherwise of Thom's findings? Was it possible to investigate the suggested Megalithic Yard? The problem was that there was still a relative absence of informed opinion regarding this subject. The situation brought to mind the words of Mr Gradgrind in Charles Dickens' *Hard Times*:

> 'Now, what I want is, Facts... Facts alone are wanted in life. Plant nothing else, and root out everything else. You can only form the minds of reasoning animals upon Facts: nothing else will ever be of any service to them... Stick to Facts, sir!'

Facts can be tricky things, as the point of view of the observer will always have a bearing on them. However, we came to the view that the only way to resolve the matter was to try to put some more facts on the table: facts that could help everyone concerned to have a more informed view. To do this we decided that we needed to try and discover how the Neolithic people could have produced the Megalithic Yard to such a high degree of accuracy across so large a geographical area and over such a long period of time. If we could find a realistic explanation of how the Megalithic unit of 0.8296656 metres could be created, it would justify a reappraisal of the existing paradigm of prehistory and potentially repair a substantial hole in the Great Wall of History.

CHAPTER 2

The Turning Earth

Does it really matter if Professor Thom was right about the Neolithic builders having used the finely-defined standard unit of length that he called the Megalithic Yard? Yes – it matters a great deal. If he was wrong, the subject of statistics needs a fundamental reappraisal; but if his findings were reliable, the subject of archaeology needs equally careful reassessment. Further – if Thom was right, the development of human civilization may have to be rewritten! We wanted to know, one way or the other: were Alexander Thom's findings real?

The truth and the Earth

There were two possibilities: either Professor Thom's Megalithic Yard was a genuine unit once used by Neolithic builders or it was an accidental consequence of statistical manipulation without any historical validity. We saw that the only hope of resolving the issue, once and for all, was to attempt to find a reason why this length of unit would have had meaning for Neolithic builders, and then to identify a methodology for reproducing such a length at different locations. It was a tall order, and failure to find a potentially meaningful origin of the Megalithic Yard and a feasible means of reproduction would still not confirm that it was a fabrication. Conversely, we recognized that success would not sufficiently prove that the measurement was real.

We have to admit that we had a starting point that suggested that Thom was correct, because Alan's previous research had led him to believe that the Megalithic Yard was, and is, a *geodetic* unit. This means that it was derived from the geometry of the Earth itself – specifically, it was based on the polar circumference of the planet.[1] After studying evidence from the Minoan culture that had developed on the Mediterranean island of Crete some 4,000 years ago, Alan had concluded that the Minoan astronomer-priests had regarded a circle as having 366 degrees rather than 360 degrees that we use today. The evidence also suggested that the Megalithic culture of Britain had done the same. Chris studied Alan's earlier findings closely and could see a logical reason why any astronomically-based culture might consider that there should be 366 degrees in a circle – for the very good reason that there are 366 rotations of the Earth in a year.

Chris's reasoning was straightforward. Everyone accepts that there are approximately 365 $1/4$ solar days in a year, and because we cannot have a quarter of a real day, our modern calendar has 365 days to the year with an extra leap day at the end of February every fourth year. There are also other subtle correctional mechanisms (for example, adding a leap year in millennium years but not in century years) designed to smooth out the oddities of the astronomical system that governs the progress of perceived time for daily purposes. While we are all relaxed about having a 365-day year, most people do not realize that the Earth actually makes just over 366 turns on its axis during the same period.

Such devoted Sun, Moon and star watchers as the Neolithic people

[1] Butler, A.: *The Bronze Age Computer Disc.* Quantum, London, 1999.

of the British Isles and surrounding areas would have been acutely aware of the difference between the 365-day year and the 366 turns of the planet in a year. One difference was the day of the Sun and the other, of the stars.

Solar and sidereal days

There are various ways of defining a day and the two principal types are what we now call a 'solar' day and a 'sidereal' day. A solar day is that measured from the zenith (the highest point) of the Sun on two consecutive days. The average time of the Sun's daily passage across the year is called a 'mean solar day' – it is this type of day that we use for our timekeeping today. A sidereal day is the time it takes for one revolution of the planet, measured by observing a star returning to the same point in the heavens on two consecutive nights. This is a real revolution because it is unaffected by the secondary motion of the Earth's orbit around the Sun. This sidereal day, or rotation period, is 236 seconds shorter than a mean solar day, and over the year these lost seconds add up to exactly one extra day, giving a year of just over 366 sidereal days in terms of the Earth's rotation about its axis.

In short, anyone who gauged the turning of Earth by watching the stars would know full well that the planet turns a little over 366 times in a year, so it follows that this number would have great significance for such star watchers. If they considered each complete turn of the Earth to be one degree of the great circle of heaven, within which the Sun, Moon and planets move, then they would also logically accept that there are 366 degrees in a circle.

There really are 366 degrees in the most important circle of them all – the Earth's yearly orbit of the Sun. Anything else is an arbitrary convention. It seemed to us that this was so logical that the 360-degree circle may have been a later adjustment to make arithmetic easier, as it is divisible by far more numbers than the 'real' number of degrees in a year. In other words, the circle of geometry has become somehow detached from the circle of heaven. How right we were, and the truth of the situation would become all too clear to us as our research progressed.

Having satisfied ourselves that Alan's conclusion about a 366-degree Neolithic circle was, at least, tenable we returned to the issue of the Megalithic Yard being a geodetically-derived concept. If it was indeed geodetic in origin it was implicit that the Neolithic peoples of western Europe had measured and understood the polar circumference of the Earth. At first view this may sound far-fetched – but it is not. In our opinion it is not unreasonable to assume that the astronomer-priests of this period did indeed achieve this feat. Few, if any, experts deny that many Megalithic sites were created for sky watching. Any culture that spent dozens of centuries studying the interplay of solar, lunar and stellar movements must surely have come to understand that the Earth is a giant ball. In the process it could quite readily have gained sufficient knowledge to gauge the Earth's size.

Given that the human brain has enjoyed its current level of intellectual processing power for tens of thousands of years, it has to be acknowledged that prehistory must have had its share of individuals with the imagination and insight of Isaac Newton or Albert Einstein. It is not outlandish, therefore, to assume that the Megalithic builders would have established the true nature of the Earth, including measuring its dimensions using simple observational astronomy. Indeed, the Greek mathematician Eratosthenes is said to have single-handedly calculated the polar circumference of the Earth in 250 BC to an accuracy of 99 percent without the considerable benefit of thousands of years of concentrated observational astronomy known to have been conducted by the people who built such sites as

Stonehenge in England.

All this deduction seemed fair but one troublesome fact did cause us to wince a little. Having decided that there was no insurmountable difficulty in measuring the polar circumference of the planet in order to subdivide it into integer (whole number) units, we had to accept that the people concerned must have possessed a reliable unit of linear measure prior to the Megalithic Yard. Some presently unknown unit simply had to be in place to measure the polar circumference before this great distance could be recalibrated into a more useful geodetic subdivision. After some thought we realized that this was not a problem at all. All we had to do was to think about the relatively recent past to understand how the history of human endeavour repeats itself if facts become lost. The 18th-century French team that devised the metric system had done exactly the same thing in that they measured the polar circumference of the Earth in old French linear units before they could create the metre, which was then defined as one forty-millionth of the circumference of the circle that passed through both poles. What 18th-century Europeans could achieve, so too could the star watchers of the Neolithic Period. But the realization does add another level of surprising expertise to these otherwise apparently unsophisticated people.

Beautiful equations

Our next question was, 'What is the modern estimate of the polar circumference of the Earth?' Given that our planet has an uneven surface and is not entirely regular in every north-south cross-section, it would appear to be almost impossible to give an absolutely precise measurement for its polar dimensions. Inevitably estimates vary slightly, but the most common value quoted is 40,008 kilometres,[2] a distance that converts to 48,221,838 Megalithic Yards (MY).

Our hypothetical 366-degree polar circumference would therefore give us 131,754 Megalithic Yards per degree – a number that does not sound very special. But Alan had reasons to believe that these early mathematicians had subdivided each degree into minutes and seconds of arc (part of the circumference of a circle), just as we do today. In this instance however, it appears they fixed upon 60 minutes to each degree of arc and 6 seconds to a minute of arc. This produced the following result:

full circle of the Earth ___ = ___ 48,221,838 MY

Well, that did not look too exciting. Nor did the next two steps:

one degree (a 366th part) ___ = ___ 131,754 MY
one minute (a 60th part) ___ = ___ 2,196 MY

But the final breakdown was truly remarkable:

one second (a 6th part) ___ = ___ 366 MY

According to this assumed system of 366-degree geometry, each second of arc of the entire planet is an amazingly precise 366 MY in length! It is incredibly neat, but is it real?

An astounding coincidence: the 'Minoan foot'

Taking Thom's Megalithic Yard of 0.8296656 metres we could reverse-engineer the process by multiplying it by 366 x 6 x 60 x 366, giving a supposed planetary circumference of a little under 40,010 kilometres. This is less than 0.005 percent away from our modern estimate and it is so close as to be negligible. While there are no decipherable records from the Neolithic Period to confirm the use of this method of geometry, there is strong circumstantial evidence to suggest that the 366 x 60 x 6 principle of geometry was used by the Minoan culture that existed on the Mediterranean Island of Crete 4,000 years ago, which overlapped the time of the Neolithic cultures of Britain and France.

Canadian archaeologist, Professor J. Walter Graham of Princeton University discovered that a standard unit of length had been employed in the design and construction of palaces on Crete dating from the Minoan period, circa 2000 BC. Graham dubbed this unit a 'Minoan foot', which he stated was equal to 30.36 centimetres.[3] This length held no particular significance for Professor Graham, as he had no reason to compare it to the units Thom claimed to have found on the other side of Europe.

It dawned on us, as we looked at Professor Graham's findings, that there was something more than significant about the size of the Minoan foot, when looked at in conjunction with the Megalithic Yard and Megalithic geometry. Imagine our surprise when we realized that one second of arc in the assumed Megalithic system (366 MY) is equal to 303.6577 metres – which is exactly 1,000 Minoan feet (given that Graham did not provide a level of accuracy greater than a tenth of a millimetre). This fit could just be a very, very strange coincidence – but it has to be noted that several researchers now believe that the Minoan culture of Crete had ongoing contact with the people who were the Megalithic builders of the British Isles.[4]

It seemed highly unlikely that 366 MY and 1,000 Minoan feet should both fit our hypothetical Megalithic Second of arc so perfectly by sheer chance, given that they both appear to spring from the same geodetically sound principle. We were now feeling increasingly confident that the Megalithic Yard was a real unit of length and not a

[2] *See*: www.earth-sci.com/Earthnmaps.html.
   See also: www.hightechscience.org; www.earth.rochester.edu
[3] Graham, J. W.: *The Palaces of Crete*. Princeton University Press, London, 1962.
[4] Castleden, R.: *The Making of Stonehenge*. Routledge, London, 1994.

statistical blip as suggested by some archaeologists – who unfortunately have never taken the time to thoroughly investigate the issue.

Having determined that the Megalithic Yard had a potential reality, there was still the problem of how it could possibly have been reproduced at tens of thousands of different sites over thousands of years. We formed a hypothesis that a group of advanced Neolithic astronomers had calculated the Megalithic Yard from a detailed knowledge of the circumference of the planet, but they would need a means of formally recording the length of the unit and of disseminating it across time and distance for general use by the builders of hundreds or thousands of individual projects.

As we have demonstrated, the modern metre was derived from the polar circumference of the Earth and it was first recorded as the distance between two fine lines engraved onto a bar made of platinum-iridium alloy. Later it was redefined in terms of the wavelength of red light from a krypton-86 source. Since 1983 the metre has been defined as the length of the path travelled by light in a vacuum during a time interval of one 299,792,458th part of a second.

We reasoned that the Megalithic Yard needed to be recorded in a way that was accessible to every builder, yet for the majority of the Megalithic Period this culture did not use metals of any kind. It is possible that two fine lines could have been cut into a rock at some significant location but such a procedure would be open to error and could not have produced the amazing accuracy found by Alexander Thom. As he himself observed, wooden measures would have been subject to damage from a host of different sources. Rather than keeping a 'sample', what our Megalithic mathematicians needed was a method of reproducing the Megalithic Yard that was simple to use, very accurate and available to people dispersed over a large distance and across a huge span of time.

A repeatable unit of measurement

It seemed to us that anyone wishing to accurately recreate the Megalithic Yard required something in the natural world that would offer them a foolproof method of recreating the subdivision of the polar dimension of the Earth that they had already established. And it had to be a process that ensured the unit of length would not change across time or physical distance. We came tantalizingly close to resolving this problem back in 1998 when Chris was putting the finishing touches to the manuscript for *Uriel's Machine*, a book he was co-authoring with Robert Lomas. At that time the three of us got together to try and find a mechanism that could have allowed Neolithic builders to reproduce a Megalithic Yard, without being given a ruler, that was accurate to less than six-tenths of a millimetre.[5]

We had reasoned that if builders separated by time and space could consistently generate the Megalithic Yard, it seemed certain that each individual had followed some well understood process in order to create their own Megalithic Yard in isolation. We proceeded by considering a shortlist of the possible candidates from nature that could conceivably offer a repeatable unit of any measurement to a human observer. This list was to prove very short indeed.

We were quickly able to dismiss all living matter as a source of consistent length. Plants and animal parts (including human limbs) vary considerably from one example to the next. We discounted minerals such as crystals because they also vary in size. After a great deal of consideration the only option seemed to lie in the heavens, which did appear to be a logical possibility because we knew that Megalithic sites had been constructed using stones carefully aligned with the Sun, the Moon and the planet Venus.

[5] Thom and Thom: *Megalithic Remains in Britain and Brittany*. Oxford University Press, Oxford, 1978. Chapters 3,4, 6, 7 & 8.

So, in the end, our shortlist of possibilities for any naturally-occurring unit of measure came down to just one candidate: the turning of the Earth on its axis – exactly the same phenomenon that we have now identified as the original justification for idea of a 366-degree circle! A real pattern was starting to emerge.

Through this careful process of elimination we had concluded that the only natural phenomenon that can be accurately measured by man is the passing of time – which, we reasoned, could best be judged by watching the apparent movement of stars. The slow motion of the stars across the night sky is simply due to the Earth turning on its axis – which is as predictable and constant as anyone could reasonably need for all practical purposes. As far as we could see there was absolutely no alternative to the revolving Earth as the basis of any unit of measurement.

Back then, we had come to the opinion that stars were a more accurate means of appreciating the turn of the Earth than any of the other heavenly bodies because of the complexity of planetary movements within the confines of the solar system. Only far later did we realize that the assumption we had made was very wrong.

Our first challenge was to puzzle over the issue of how any unit of time could possibly be converted into a linear unit. Here we took a leaf from Professor Thom's book and attempted to design our own solution to the problem that we assumed once confronted the Megalithic builders. If we could produce a method that worked for us, we reasoned, we could then compare our result with evidence from the Megalithic sites.

In order to become acclimatized to the problem we ventured out onto the Yorkshire moors in northern England on a cold, starry night to soak up the dramatic majesty of the heavens that swing over the heads of all humanity once each day. The human eye is a remarkably adaptable light detector, able to function in bright sunlight and still pick up faint starlight. With practice it is possible to see deep space objects such as the Andromeda galaxy, and in doing so we are observing light that left that faint smudge in the heavens some two million years ago – a period before our distant ancestors, *Homo erectus*, first stood upright!

We pondered the difficulty of turning the apparent motion of the stars into units of time without the benefit of a stopwatch. Today we take the concept of time for granted because we have clocks and wrist-watches to synchronize our lives, but most of us forget that the hours, minutes and seconds we use are themselves only a convenient and artificial way of monitoring the spin of our planet.

The pendulum

Measuring time is a real problem today, let alone more than 5,000 years ago. We now needed to try and work out how to create units of time from the spinning of the Earth on its axis, using only the technology available to the people of the late Stone Age. It seemed tough, but we eventually realized that the answer lay in a pendulum.

At the heart of a traditional clock lies the pendulum. The wind-up spring or electrical motor is merely a mechanical device to provide a power source to keep the pendulum swinging rather than have to swing it by hand. And the dial on the clockface is simply a convention to give us a standardized means of reading off agreed units of time. When we stripped away the modern aspects of a mechanical clock we realized that it is, in essence, nothing more than a swinging pendulum.

We could imagine that a hypothetical Megalithic clock could work perfectly well without a clockwork mechanism or a dial. All we needed to create such a timepiece was for two of us to take turns to swing a pebble on the end of a piece of twine with our hands while the other counted off groups of completed beats. For example, a small stone could be put in a line for every 100 beats. This 'man-clock' would work well enough to allow for very accurate astronomical calculations to be carried out over several days if necessary.

The time that it takes a pendulum to swing is governed by just two factors: the mass of the Earth and the length of the pendulum from the fulcrum (the point at which it is held and pivots) to the centre of gravity of the weight. Nothing else is of significant importance. The amount of effort that the person holding the pendulum puts into the swing has no bearing on the time per swing because a more powerful motion will produce a wider arc and a higher speed of travel, whereas a low power swing will cause the weight to travel less distance at a reduced speed. Equally, the heaviness of the weight of the object on the end of the line is immaterial – a heavier or lighter weight will simply change the speed/distance ratio without having any effect on the time of the swing.

The mass of the Earth is a constant factor, although there are tiny variations of the acceleration due to gravity at different latitudes and altitudes because the Earth bulges slightly at the equator, causing a minute change in the angle to the Earth's core. However, in an area the size of the British Isles anyone swinging a pendulum for a known number of swings in a fixed period of time will have almost exactly the same pendulum length.

Pendulums certainly seemed like prime candidates. It was self-evident to us that the builders of the stone circles possessed such objects because they could not have erected their perfectly vertical standing stones without them.

A pendulum is nothing more than a swinging plumb line. All that was required was a regular-shaped weight on the end of a piece of twine – and certainly many pebbles with holes drilled through their centres have been found at these ancient sites. These are usually described as

A simple pendulum

'loom-weights' used in the weaving of cloth, but some could equally well be the remnants of plumb lines.

When we first looked at this problem with Robert Lomas we had outlined a technique of measuring the rotation of the Earth by standing in the centre of a large circle and watching a star pass between two pillars that were spaced to be one 366th of the circle of the horizon. We found that we could produce a pendulum length that was very close to a half Megalithic Yard by swinging the pendulum 366 times during the passage of the star. The swings required were actually closer to $365^1/_2$ but we reasoned that the user would have counted the last swing in full.

The morning star

Long after our joint investigation with Robert Lomas in this exercise was over, we returned to the issue of the small discrepancy between

Thom's Megalithic Yard and our pendulum-based result. The process we had identified seemed too close to be plain wrong and yet what amounted to a half pendulum swing niggled away at the pair of us. The more we thought about it, the more we felt we had missed something very significant. We decided to investigate every possible option including the use of the Sun, Moon and the planets as indicators of the passage of time. Ultimately we found our candidate and, once we did, we kicked ourselves for not having recognized it all along. It was the planet Venus that our ancient ancestors had used to calibrate their pendulum and therefore keep the size of the Megalithic Yard absolutely accurate.

A star, being millions of kilometres distant from our solar system, will always appear to occupy the same place in the sky when seen from Earth (except over vast amounts of time, which need not concern us here). But planets are a different matter. Like the Earth, planets are orbiting the Sun and so when seen from the Earth, they have movement that is independent of what we call the fixed stars. This situation is similar to a stage on which a play is going to take place. The stage, with its scenery, is like the starry backdrop we see every night, while the actors can be equated with the planets, which can move independently of the stage scenery.

As the Earth turns on its axis once each day, so the stars appear to turn over our heads. There is one band of stars, known as 'the plane of the ecliptic', through which the Sun, Moon and planets of the solar system appear to travel. Historically, this band was split into 12 sections, known as the zodiac. Patterns or 'constellations' of stars in each of the sections were thought to look like some animal, person or object and it is from this we derive the different names of the zodiac signs.

We might stand and look to the east on a particular night in the year and see the constellation of Aries rising over the eastern horizon.

As the night progresses it would be replaced by Taurus, then Gemini, Cancer, Leo and so on, until one sidereal day later, when Aries would appear again. Against this backdrop we would see the planets which, in addition to seemingly follow the stars, are also slowly progressing through the zodiac constellations. The speed with which the planets appear to us to pass through the zodiac depends partly on their distance from the Sun but is also modified by the fact that we are on the Earth, which is also going around the Sun. Because of this 'line of sight' effect, the planets can sometimes even appear to move backwards within the zodiac.

Planetary movements can seem tortuously difficult to understand, particularly those of a planet such as Venus, which is closer to the Sun than is the Earth. From our perspective Venus can be either a 'morning star' in which case it rises before dawn and therefore ahead of the Sun, or it can be an evening star, in which case it is still visible in the sky after the Sun has set (though of course it isn't a star at all, even if it looks like one). But no matter whether it is a morning or evening star, it still moves through the zodiac signs, independent of the stars.

There are periods in each Venus 'cycle' when it achieves a speed within the zodiac of as much as 1 degree and 16 seconds of arc per day. Since this movement is opposite to the movement of the stars themselves, Venus will take more than a full sidereal day to pass from a particular point on the horizon to that same point again.

We then had to think about our original Megalithic pendulum experiment in which we observed a star passing between two pillars with the sides angled to be at 90 degrees to the path of the stars. If we used Venus instead of a star, there would be times in each of its cycles when it would take longer to pass between the posts than would a star. We discovered that this 'time-lag' was just enough to account for the missing half-swing of our pendulum.

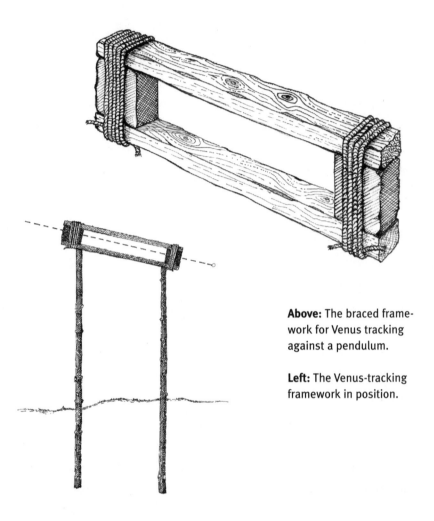

Above: The braced framework for Venus tracking
against a pendulum.

Left: The Venus-tracking
framework in position.

The technique required was very straightforward. A circle had to be
constructed from a centre pole using a rope before dividing the
perimeter into 366 sections. This could be done by trial and error or by
using a trick of geometry: making the diameter 233 units across (any
unit will do) and then measuring off 2 units on the circumference. The
pendulum bearer would then stand in the middle of the circle while a
colleague erected a square frame that had an internal dimension equal
to one Megalithic degree. The square was adjusted until the pendulum

bearer confirmed that its top and bottom were aligned with the passage of Venus.

The bearer then started swinging the pendulum when Venus appeared inside the square and stopped when it disappeared again. There was no likelihood of error since it is clear that these sky watchers knew to check Venus on a regular basis. Because Venus sometimes moves faster within the zodiac than at other times, the very longest half Megalithic Yard pendulum achievable within the Venus cycle was the one they were looking for.

If the bearer had been able to count exactly 366 swings, they knew they had confirmed their pendulum as being a half Megalithic Yard. If the count was short, they repeated the process after reducing the length and, conversely, the length would be increased if too many swings had occurred.

There is no doubt about it. Our Megalithic ancestors calibrated their half Megalithic Yard pendulum not using a star, but the planet Venus. We berated ourselves for not hitting upon the Venus method earlier because both of our respective earlier researches have involved this planet. Chris had already shown that, in a ritualistic sense, Venus had been of stunning importance to the Megalithic peoples as well as later groups such as the Babylonians, the Canaanites and latterly, the Jews.[6]

The importance of Venus

Working with Robert Lomas, Chris has published findings that demonstrate the huge importance of Venus to the builders of the Megalithic sites in the British Isles. The gigantic and very beautiful 5,000-year-old observatory at Newgrange was painstakingly designed to let the light of Venus into the central chamber for only minutes once every eight years

[6] Knight, C. and Lomas, R.: *The Book of Hiram*. Arrow, London, 2004.

on the winter solstice.[7] This and other sites would have enabled the Neolithic astronomers to maintain a completely accurate calendar. Chris had also argued that there was reason to believe that the light of Venus was considered to be involved with birth and resurrection. This is because the internal design of Newgrange appears to have been constructed to emulate female reproductive organs and the light of Venus penetrates the passageway like a celestial phallus. Such mating between heaven and Earth was not an uncommon concept in ancient traditions and according to the Roman historians the later Celts are said to have conducted copulation rituals at the spring equinox and women gave birth at the winter solstice – just as a shaft of light from Venus exploded into the centre of the huge structure. At that very point is a lone carving depicting three interlaced spirals, which represented nine months – the gestation period of a human female.

Meanwhile, we both knew just how important Venus had been to a range of ancient civilizations, not least because the orbits of Venus act as a natural calendar reference for the Earth itself. There is a relationship between Earth and Venus that was always seen as being deeply mystical, in that five periods of Venus are the same as eight Earth years.

From Alan's point of view, the realization that Venus could act as the necessary pendulum-setter came as direct proof of the validity of his own earlier discoveries regarding the Phaistos Disc. The Phaistos Disc is a 6 centimetre baked clay disc, found in the ruins of the Minoan Palace of Phaistos in Crete. It dates back to the Minoan civilization (circa 2000 BC). Appendix 5 gives a great deal more information about the Phaistos Disc and includes drawings of the artefact. For the moment it is sufficient to say that this amazing little disc is a multifaceted calculating machine, based on the Megalithic 366-day year. One

---

[7] Knight, C. and Lomas, R.: *Uriel's Machine*. Arrow, London, 2000.

of the jobs it performs is to indicate to those using this year when to compensate for the difference between the ritual year of 366 days and the true solar year of 365.25 days. However, the disc does more than this because it also provides the mathematical framework for establishing the position of Venus in the zodiac on *any* day – *ever*. It does this in a very simple way, explained in Appendix 5, but the fact remains that Venus tracking is an essential part of the abilities of this little calculator.

When the Venus experiment was undertaken in Orkney, Scotland, where some of the most magnificent of the Megalithic monuments are to be found, the size of the resulting pendulum was very significant. The pendulum would prove to be a half Megalithic Yard, the full length of which would deviate from Alexander Thom's findings by a staggering 1 part in 2,700. Allowing for the human factor (that someone has to hold the pendulum and decide when to start and stop it) the Venus-based half Megalithic Yard pendulum was perfect. Our result was within the very fine margin of error identified by Professor Thom.

This method of reproducing the Megalithic Yard was so simple it was not even necessary for the master mason to count the number of beats in any modern sense. Counting does not have to be part of a tiered system such as the base ten method used today, in which we add up in multiples of ten by adding a nought after the digit. A nursery rhyme or a sea shanty is a good way of counting out a set number without understanding arithmetic. For example, reciting the following passage while pointing at a sheep for each word will tell you whether your flock of 20 is still intact:

'Eeny, meeny, miney, mow, catch a monkey by the toe. If he squeals let him go. Eeny, meeny, miney, mow.'

It follows that measuring something as simple as this could be as old as language itself. Indeed, the words 'eeny, meeny, miney, mow' are thought to be an ancient British counting technique from more than 4,000 years ago.

Beyond reasonable doubt

There is no doubt that the Megalithic Yard is a superb integer of the polar circumference of the Earth – right down to a second of arc that is an incredible 366 Megalithic Yards in length. Once this unit had been defined by obviously gifted astronomers, these early scientists appear to have created a foolproof method that every master mason could use to generate an accurate Megalithic Yardstick.

This whole process is brilliantly simple, memorable and unerringly accurate. Of course there will have been errors of judgement when transferring the length from the pendulum to a measuring stick but that is the kind of distribution of error that Alexander Thom found. Because there was a physical reality behind the process, all errors deviated from a central point of 82.96656 centimetres. Pure Neolithic genius!

After several years of intense investigation we had come to a point where there were only three basic possibilities for Alexander Thom's Megalithic Yard:

1. The unit that Thom thought he had detected at hundreds of Megalithic sites was an error of statistical manipulation. The fact that the unit he defined, to within a 10,000th of a millimetre, just happened to so precisely fit the Earth's circumference and was reproducible using the astronomically key number of 366 were both coincidences. It followed that the hypothetical 366-degree geometry system outlined was not real

and the precise fit of 366 Megalithic Yards and 1,000 Minoan feet to an assumed second of arc was a further coincidence.

2. Thom's Megalithic Yard was real in some still unknown way and our interpretation only fitted the facts by sheer coincidence.

3. We had rediscovered the wonderful system that was used to define and recreate the Megalithic Yard.

It is up to each reader to come to their own conclusion as to which option is most likely to be correct. At this stage we were fully convinced that the first two options were not correct because of the number of outrageous coincidences required to sustain either view. However, little did we know that we had barely scratched the surface of a system that makes all modern approaches to measurement look simply crude. We had just begun on a journey that was to tap into the very fabric of the universe.

In solving the riddle of the Megalithic Yard we believe we have made it easy for archaeologists to at last accept Thom's findings without any fundamental contradiction of their existing views on the abilities of the builders of the Megalithic structures of western Europe. But now it looked as though there was a far deeper understanding of astronomy behind the creation of the Megalithic Yard than anyone could have imagined and the world of academic archaeology is likely to resist the idea that the Neolithic astronomers could have achieved so much. We share their surprise, but the balance of probabilities makes the continued rejection of Thom's conclusion unscientific and merely the result of personal prejudice.

One leading academic was brave enough to be generous about our early attempt to solve the mystery of the Megalithic Yard. In September 2000 Chris and Robert Lomas attended the Orkney Science Festival where they shared our first, albeit slightly flawed explanation of the Megalithic Yard with Archie Roy, Emeritus Professor of Astronomy at Glasgow University. Professor Roy is not only a distinguished astronomer but he had also worked with Professor Thom in identifying the archaeoastronomy present in Megalithic sites. He spent the evening checking the mathematics involved in our original model, based upon the movement of stars, and the next morning he announced that the method did work in principle. He then joined Chris and Robert in a public demonstration of how the Megalithic Yard might have been created. Professor Roy added that he believed we had opened up a new chapter in the understanding of Megalithic Man.

Alexander Thom had never attempted to justify his findings in cultural terms. He did not believe it was for him to explain how or why the Neolithic inhabitants of western Europe developed the Megalithic Yard – like the true engineer he was he simply reported what the data showed. Those who wanted to construct a smooth model of prehistory were not happy because of the consequences of accepting that the Stone Age builders were actually very sophisticated. It was simply too inconvenient to even consider a re-evaluation of the standard credo concerning human development.

The result is that few people of reputable scientific standing have looked afresh at the late Stone Age and early Bronze Age cultures in and around the British Isles. The archaeologists gaze at their recovered physical artefacts and they see a consistent picture – but maybe it is only consistent because they ignore evidence that does not suit their model. Now we have established that the Megalithic builders were, beyond all reasonable doubt, using a highly sophisticated system of measurement despite the fact that every other piece of evidence suggests that they were not generally very advanced.

There seemed to be two possible scenarios: either these Neolithic people were very accomplished surveyors and astronomers or they had accidentally stumbled upon some important natural phenomenon when they based their common unit of linear length on the dimensions of the Earth. Perhaps they did not understand what was happening – but then how could the Minoans have employed the same principle in a different application if the whole thing was an accident?

This is real!

A very strange picture was beginning to emerge and it seemed sensible to search for any other evidence that might be available. If the Megalithic people were smart enough to develop a complex system of geometry, we had to assume that they could have done more. Having created their unit of length from a unit of time, the next obvious steps would have been to create units of weight and capacity. Such a move would have been an important building block towards trade, which was in turn a key step towards true civilization.

It seemed to us that if an integrated system of weights had once existed around the '366' concept, the best route forward would be to continue to use Thom's principle of asking the question, 'What would I have done to achieve the assumed goal?' Taking this simple philosophy Chris began a series of experiments that gave results that were to be as shocking as they were totally perplexing.

Conclusions

◎ We have been able to demonstrate that the Megalithic Yard was real, being derived directly from the polar circumference of the Earth using a system of geometry that was based on the number of revolutions of the planet in a year.

◎ When we compared Professor Thom's findings with those of Professor Graham relating to the Minoan foot, we found that both appear to be based on this highly sophisticated system of Earth geometry that assumed a circle of 366 degrees. The precision of the geometric correlation between these apparently unrelated ancient units causes us to take as proven the pre-existence of the system where a second of arc of the polar equator is respectively equal to 366 Megalithic Yards and 1,000 Minoan feet.

◎ We also identified a simple method whereby anyone given simple instructions could repeatedly and accurately create the Megalithic Yard using only basic tools and straightforward observational astronomy.

CHAPTER 3

The Harmony of the Spheres

Megalithic society

We have to concede that the society that existed at the building of the Megalithic structures in the British Isles does seem too primitive to have developed a precise system of measurement. The lives of these people must have been difficult, involving a permanent struggle to produce food and keep warm. So little is known about the inhabitants of these islands in these truly ancient times that they are remembered by the style of the pottery they left behind. Some earlier groups are now known as the Grooved Ware people and Unstan Ware people, with later representatives of the Megalithic culture designated the Beaker Folk. All these terms refer to specific designs or shapes of vessels created by the cultures or subcultures in question and archaeological finds are often dated with reference to pottery shards.

The main upsurge in building began around the middle of the fourth millennium BC when the climate of the British Isles was warmer and wetter than it is today and with a slightly longer growing season. It is known that inhabitants of the region cultivated wheat and barley because impressions of these cereals have been found on pottery fragments. Such printings are evident in examples from across much of Europe and Asia and the cereal grains may be been deliberately used to add patterns to prehistoric pottery. We were to discover that grain seeds, and those of barley especially, had a practical as well as a ritual significance to our ancient ancestors.

These early farmers ploughed the ground with animal bones and planted seeds using a simple kind of mattock or hoe before harvesting their crops with flint sickles and using flat querns (grinding stones) to grind the grain. Experts believe that it must have been a very wasteful process by any later standards. The Grooved Ware people knew nothing of crop rotation and when the ground was exhausted, the farmers moved on, clearing the next patch of woodland with stone axes and burning off the remaining scrub.

Hunted species included deer and wild cattle and available marine resources comprised freshwater and sea fish, especially shellfish including oysters, winkles, cockles, crabs, and razor-shells. Besides planted crops, wild plant resources, including fruits, roots, hazelnuts and acorns were gathered, and rope was manufactured from fibrous plants such as heather, which was twisted. Husbanded livestock included sheep, cows, goats, pigs and dogs, which are believed to have been introduced from mainland Europe between 4200–3500 BC. The evidence from all the settlement sites suggests that sheep or goats and cattle were kept in approximately equal proportions but pigs were relatively rare.

Movement across the countryside for these first British farmers was difficult due to thick forest cover and marshes and, significantly, because the wheel was unknown in western Europe at this time. Heavy loads were moved using land sledges and rafts. Water must have provided the best means of transport and experts have suggested that small animal-skin boats rather like the Inuit whaling umiak or the Irish curragh were used.

Stone tools made from flint, chert beach pebbles and rum bloodstone were used and polished stone axe heads were manufactured in Ireland from around 4000 BC, before spreading to the rest of the British Isles. The dwellings excavated from the period are rectilinear timber structures with stone bases and turf roofs, typically about 6 x 6 metres, although they were sometimes much larger.

The astronomer-priests

The lives these people led were basic but it is almost certain that amongst them existed a class that was different from the norm. Its existence was made possible because of surplus food production and specialization of crafts and trades. These people, thinkers and proto-engineers, doubtless supervised the building of the impressive Megalithic structures that Alexander Thom could understand thousands of years later. As hunter-gatherers, the whole community would have been involved in the daily struggle to find food and make new homes as they moved from place to place. With the advent of farming, the culture could afford to create the considerable support structure needed to cut deep henges (circular ditches), sometimes out of solid rock and to construct giant structures like Newgrange in Ireland. By this stage, many people must have been permanently involved with building and these individuals had to be fed, clothed and housed by the efforts of others. The nature of the finished sites clearly demonstrates that an elite had emerged which represented the architects, the scientists, the thinkers and, no doubt, the poets. These were the 'magi' – the astronomer-priests who had responsibility for designing and building the Megalithic sites that Professor Thom studied so closely.

It also appears that there might have been a national network of Megalithic observatories with different ones being used for varying astronomical purposes dependent on the location of each. Had these structures been made to satisfy purely local or religious needs, one would expect to see less commonality in the style and layout than is evident across a very extensive area.

One archaeological site found at Skara Brae in Orkney is particularly interesting because it may well have been a Megalithic 'university' for training astronomer-priests. Radiocarbon dating has shown that it was occupied between approximately 3215–2655 BC when it provided a series of linked rooms, each with matching stone-built furniture including dressers, beds, cooking areas and sealed stone water tubs for washing. Archaeologists have identified that secrecy, security and plumbing are also apparent at the site. A secret hidey-hole has been found under the stone dresser and a hole for a locking bar was located on both sides of doors. In addition, a lavatory drain designed to run excrement along wooden piping and into the sea has also been excavated. Curiously, the house designated by archaeologists as 'number seven' was isolated and its door was barred from the outside suggesting that it was designed to house an occupant being kept against their will.

The archaeologist Euan Mackie first put forward the idea that Skara Brae had been a kind of prehistoric college when he noticed that the remains of the sheep and cows eaten there had far too few skulls for the number of carcasses. He concluded that pre-butchered meat had been imported to the island, along with the firewood required to cook it.[1] Because the island had nothing to trade, the only reasonable answer to this archaeological puzzle is that the inhabitants had been an elite group who where supported by the goodwill of a broader community at a distance.

[1] Mackie, E.: *The Megalithic Builders*. Phaidon Press, London, 1977.

Skara Brae also revealed some artefacts that have proved impossible to understand. Small stone objects that have been exquisitely carved include two balls: one 6.2 centimetres and the other 7.7 centimetres in diameter. Their purpose is unknown and the deep decoration appears to be impossible to create without metal tools as engineer James Macauley discovered when he attempted to reproduce them using the known technology of the time.

Weights and measures

If we had begun our quest by creating intellectual boundaries relating to what was and was not feasible for this culture to achieve, we would never have found the solution to the Megalithic Yard. However, we had been very impressed with the unit, the method for proving it and also its wide distribution, which indicated common values and perhaps religious beliefs. With this in mind Chris took another speculative step forward and began to construct a theoretical weight and capacity system to accompany that of time, distance and geometry that we had already established. He started at the point in history at which many more modern cultures appear to have started when creating such units; by making a cube and filling it with water. Chris knew that those creating the metric system had opted for a length of one tenth of a metre, which they cubed. The volume of water in such a 10 x 10 x 10 centimetre cube was designated a litre, and the weight of such a body of water was named a kilogram.

In our case, the linear units would have to be in Megalithic Inches, which Thom identified as being one fortieth of a Megalithic Yard, equal to 2.07415 centimetres. Taking his lead from the metric system Chris first considered a cube with sides of a tenth of a Megalithic Yard – i.e. four Megalithic Inches (MI). In metric terms this turned out to have a capacity of a little over half a litre, at 571.08 cubic centimetres.

The 'imperial system'

As he performed the simple sum on his calculator Chris thought he recognized the number produced and he quickly converted it into imperial units (the standard measuring system still used in Britain). His brow furrowed and he repeated the calculation twice more to confirm his result. Something very odd was happening because the theoretical Megalithic unit of capacity was equal to 1.005 pints – far closer to one perfect British pint than any pub landlord achieves when pulling a glass of draught ale! Of course, this had to be a coincidence, but it was a really surprising one nonetheless. Next, he doubled the length of the side of the cube to 8 MI and the shock of the first coincidence was compounded because this calculation produced a capacity of one imperial gallon to the same incredible level of accuracy. A doubling again produced a unit equivalent to an obsolete bushel, which was used as a dry weight until as recently as the 1970s.

As Chris stopped to think about the calculations he realized that the gallon would have to fit the same way as the pint because there are eight pints to a gallon and a doubling of the side of a cube will create a capacity eight times larger. But this fact did not detract from the oddity because the imperial system is not known to be based on cubes. These results were odd in the extreme and all logic said that they had to be a coincidence. We had already learned not to dismiss any information simply because it does not fit our own preconceptions. So, instead of tossing the calculation in his office bin Chris picked up the phone and told Alan about the strange correspondence.

'What?' Alan responded. 'That's crazy!'

'I'm not saying there is a connection – it has to be a coincidence because the pint and the gallon as we know them today are medieval units at best, and they have probably been restandardized several times,' Chris explained.

But he went on to suggest that we could not simply ignore the results, just because they seemed ridiculous. We should not rule out the possibility that there was some sort of oddball connection between the Megalithic Yard and the imperial measurements, and added, 'Though I have no idea what it might be.'

We quickly established that the pint and the gallon had had a variety of values before the standardization of imperial units in the various British Weights and Measures Acts of the 19th century, so the correspondence with the Megalithic cube might not be meaningful. However, we looked at examples of the pint from earlier periods and found only small variations. One that was almost the same as the imperial pint dated from the reign of Henry VII (1485–1509) and checking this against the 4 Megalithic Inch cube showed that it was even closer than the modern pint. It was almost a perfect match, with a deviation of less than 1 part in a 1,000. Closer still was the standard pint identified for the Exchequer of the British government in the year 1601 because it had an amazing correspondence with the 4 Megalithic Inch – being out by less than 1 part in 5,000. To all intents and purposes this Elizabethan pint and the volume of the Megalithic cube are the same thing.

The pint had turned out to be much older than we imagined and early examples show an almost incredible correspondence to our Megalithic cube. What it meant we didn't know, but we agreed to accept the volumetric findings without judgement and continued to look at the subject in greater depth.

The next day Chris rang Alan again with some important news.

'You know we agreed to look at this area of theoretical Megalithic volumes without self-imposed boundaries, don't you?'

Alan had learned to anticipate Chris's puzzlement or excitement.

'Yes,' he confirmed. 'So what have you found now?'

'Well, I thought for thoroughness I ought to consider the volumes of spheres with Megalithic dimensions in addition to the cubes. This sounds really crazy, and I want you to check this out, but I think we have a problem.'

'What sort of problem?' Alan wanted to know.

'The problem of explaining the apparently impossible,' said Chris. 'I started by checking out spheres with diameters of 5, 10 and 20 Megalithic Inches and they also produce volumes that are quite close to the pint, one gallon and the bushel. The accuracy level isn't quite as good as the cubes because the 5 MI sphere held 1.027 pints, which is still as close as anyone in the real world would ever need. But a quick check of the rules that govern the relationship between cubes and spheres revealed that to an accuracy of 99.256 percent a cube with a side of 4 units will have the same volume as a sphere with a diameter of 5 units, which made the findings odd but mathematically understandable.'

Alan was intrigued but puzzled.

'If there is no mystery about the pint sphere, why did you say you had to explain the impossible?' he asked.

'What I've told you so far is the easy part of this conversation, because my next test took me from the rather weird to the downright ridiculous. What do you think that a 6 MI and a 60 MI diameter sphere would hold in terms of weight of water?'

'I can't guess. What do they hold?' Alan asked, with not a little impatience.

'Well, the 6 MI sphere holds a litre and weighs a kilo, so the 60 MI sphere, 10 x 10 x 10 times as much, holds a cubic metre and weighs a metric tonne. And it's incredibly accurate too.'

Alan laughed aloud down the phone.

'Ha ha, very funny...' He paused. 'You are joking, aren't you?'

'No. You check it out, Alan. The numbers don't lie. The fit is better than 99 percent accurate and when I tested the same principles using modern inches and centimetres for the spheres, there were no meaningful results at all. Something truly weird is going on here.'

Alan ran through the calculations during the conversation and agreed that they were correct. The fact that units of Megalithic linear measurement so accurately produce modern imperial measures of capacity when cubed was a fascinating coincidence, but the spheres were something else altogether. For it to be a further massive coincidence seemed almost impossible, yet for there to be a connection seemed even more unlikely.

The possibility of a random event in this case seemed minute because the formula for finding the volume of a sphere (see Appendix 2) involves the concept of pi (π), which is the relationship between the diameter and circumference of a circle. Pi is an irrational number (that is, one that cannot be expressed as a whole fraction) equal to 3.14159265359…, but the numbers after the decimal point apparently go on forever in a seemingly random stream of digits. This makes it very odd indeed that there could be a correspondence between the metric system and spheres that have Megalithic dimensions, not least because the metric system was not developed until the end of the 18th century!

At this point, we had two options: either to forget the whole matter as some bizarre chance event, or to continue investigating the whole area without passing judgement. We chose the latter course, managing to convince each other that the results might make sense with more evidence and the passage of time.

The Megalithic pint cube

Alan started to wonder what substances the Megalithic people might have wanted to weigh if they had devised a system of weights and measures. He knew that it was within the bounds of the available technology of these people to create a square vessel to form a cube because sealed water containers had been found at Skara Brae. Having manufactured his own 4 x 4 x 4 MI cube the obvious first thought was grain, specifically barley and wheat. He managed to get hold of some seeds of ancient strains and began to conduct practical experiments with his 'Megalithic pint cube'. He quickly discovered that all grains, whether barley, wheat or unpolished rice, behave in a very predictable way when poured into a cube container. The pointed, ellipsoid shape of the seeds causes them to occupy a volume that is 125 percent that of the same weight of water, bearing in mind that the relative densities of water and seed are different. Alan filled his pint cube with barley grains as carefully as possible and then tipped them out onto the pan of a pair of scales to weigh the result. The barley grains weighed exactly one imperial pound!

Further experiments with an 8 x 8 x 8 MI cube filled with barley confirmed that it weighed 8 pounds and the 16 x 16 x 16 weighed 1 bushel – a known dry weight of 64 pounds.

This was truly incredible. A pint of water and a pound of grain both appeared to be derived from a cube with sides one tenth of a Megalithic Yard long.

Like everyone in our society, we have been taught that the pound and the pint are old units. However, nobody suggests these are 'ancient' units of measure, and we were also aware that standardization to precise current values of both the pound and the pint is a relatively recent event. Yet, if we put aside our own prejudices and looked at the evidence as an objective outsider might, we could see the conclusion staring us in the face. Stretching credibility, we could imagine what might have happened in Neolithic Britain.

At some point in the distant past when trade was developing, someone had created a system of weights and measures using the Megalithic Yard and Megalithic Inches as a starting point. Taking a length of one tenth of a Megalithic Yard as the internal dimension they carefully cut five thin pieces of slate and sealed the joints with fine clay. This innovator had then filled the cube with water until the meniscus was bowing at the rim. Next they poured off the water into a clay beaker and marked the water line on the inside to create a standard unit of liquid that just happens to be the same as an imperial pint. A further procedure was to fill the same cube with grain, gently patting the top to ensure that it was as level as possible within the cube. Our imaginary scientist then poured the grain onto a simple balance and chipped shavings from a stone on the opposite side until the scales were in equilibrium. This stone was thereafter a standard unit of weight that, once again, just happens to be the same as an imperial unit – the modern pound. This hypothetical early trader thus could have created accurate and repeatable units of liquid measure and dry weight simply by watching the motion of Venus crossing the heavens. What a magical thought!

If the pound and the pint were really Megalithic, the parallels between the Megalithic and the metric systems were quite astonishing. Both basic linear units were based on a subdivision of the polar circumference of the Earth, and both units of weight and capacity were defined by a cube with sides one tenth of the linear unit.

The pound and the pint could be recreated anywhere by anyone with the necessary knowledge to watch Venus travel across one 366th part of the sky and swing their pendulum the required number of times. By any reasonable definition these were divine units taken straight from heaven. There was no magic in this, just science, and what is more, science as pure and perfect as it would ever be need to be to create a springboard for civilization.

Now, we asked ourselves again, is all this perfection just chance? Any normal academic would have run away from these findings long before they had reached this point, in fear of so much ridicule from peers that it could spell the effective end of a career. But we are not constrained by such pressures and we had arrived at a point at which it would have been unreasonable to reject the thesis that had unfolded in front of us.

How could this intricate and delightful paradigm be an illusion?

We now felt that we had almost accidentally opened an ancient door that was letting in some brilliant light. Despite the fact that we could not begin to think of a mechanism that could connect the Megalithic builders with modern units such as the pound and pint, and the kilogram and litre, we felt sure that there was something very special happening here.

The modern pound is correctly called the 'avoirdupois pound'. It is believed to have been first introduced by the counts of Champagne for use at the fairs in 12th-century France. The meaning of the word 'avoirdupois' is somewhat obscure but it could relate to Old French and simply mean 'objects of weight'. For more than 150 years, approximately 1140–1320, the fairs of Champagne constituted the international centre of European commerce, credit and currency exchange. Champagne was an agriculturally-rich region north and east of Paris, with a large and affluent population. The principal fairs were held in four cities in the southwest of the province: Lagny, Provins, Troyes, and Bar-sur-Aube.

The fairs were mostly wholesale operations with merchants buying and selling among themselves, rather than selling in a retail sense. They are further distinguished from normal markets by their great duration and by their infrequency. These great fairs lasted five weeks or more, and only the city of Troyes had more than one in a year. Many of the products traded were agricultural in nature and the term 'avoirdupois' is thought by some to have indicated anything sold by weight, such as spices, metals and dyes.

The rod

Where the counts of Champagne obtained their avoirdupois pound is not known and we agreed to return to this issue when we had gathered more information. Chris decided to look more closely at all modern measurements to see if there were any other notable correlations with Megalithic units. The imperial system is said to have evolved from disparate units from the past, involving body parts such as palm-widths, feet and outstretched arms. The standard imperial units of length still in use, or used in very recent times, form the following table:

12 inches	= 1 foot
3 feet	= 1 yard
$5^1/_2$ yards	= 1 rod
4 rods	= 1 chain
10 chains	= 1 furlong
8 furlongs	= 1 mile

As Chris looked at this now almost redundant list for the first time since he left primary school, he felt that the sequence appeared chaotic and that the rod stood out as being particularly odd at $5^1/_2$ yards or $16^1/_2$ feet. While the other units were neat integer numbers, the rod gave the impression of being alien – as though it had come from somewhere else. As he considered the rod (also known as a pole or a perch) he noticed that it was very close to six Megalithic Yards. In fact the rod is 6 Megalithic Yards to an accuracy of 99 percent. Could it be, Chris wondered, that the rod was an ancient Megalithic unit? For thoroughness, he tried the rod as a potential metric unit and the surprises continued because it was 5 metres – to an accuracy greater than 99.5 percent. Both of these could easily be a coincidence but the question that sprang to mind was, 'Had the rod once been an ancient unit that was tidied up to equal 16.5 feet at some point in the relatively recent past?' He could see a hypothetical underlying Megalithic pattern that would make a lot more sense:

40 Megalithic Inches	= 1 Megalithic Yard
6 Megalithic Yards	= 1 Megalithic Rod

4 rods	= 1 chain	
10 chains	= 1 furlong	(40 rods = 1 furlong)
8 furlongs	= 1 mile	(320 rods = 1 mile)

A sequence of 40 – 6 – 4 – 10 – 8 looked far more logical than the standard explanation and it required only a tiny adjustment to the modern definition of the rod to achieve it. This was highly speculative thinking but it was producing some very interesting results. Next Chris tried introducing his theoretical Megalithic Rod into the metric system:

10 millimetres	= 1 centimetre
100 centimetres	= 1 metre
5 metres	= 1 rod
200 rods	= 1 kilometre

The hypothetical Megalithic Rod was amazingly accurate in its fit and entirely logical. Nevertheless, we had to remind ourselves that its relationship with the metre could not be real because the metric system was not invented until the closing years of the 18th century. Or so we thought at the time!

The results suggested that the mile and the kilometre could both be units that developed from the hypothetical Megalithic Rod:

1 mile	= 1920 MY	= 320 Megalithic Rods
1 kilometre	= 1200 MY	= 200 Megalithic Rods

So both the modern mile and the kilometre are related to each other by the use of the Megalithic Yard and an assumed Megalithic Rod. (Not to be confused with the length that Alexander Thom called a Megalithic Rod. Alexander Thom had identified a unit of 2.5 Megalithic Yards, used on many of the sites he surveyed. He had christened this the Megalithic Rod.) According to standard conversions there are 1.6093 kilometres to a mile and this Megalithic approach gives a relationship between the two that is almost perfect.

Next Chris considered the imperial unit of area – the acre, which is defined as 4,840 square yards. He quickly found that it made a great deal more sense when viewed in Megalithic terms because it represents 5,760 square Megalithic Yards which is a very logical 4 x 40 Megalithic Rods. It can also be expressed as 360 packets of land each 4 x 4 MY.

Looking into now obsolete imperial units Chris also discovered that until recently there was something known as a 'square rod' which is defined as being a rather oddball $30^1/_4$ square yards. The Megalithic Rod once again made sense of it because it was an exact 36 square Megalithic Yards.

The key to a lost reality

Suddenly the imperial method was looking like a specially designed system based on the Megalithic Yard, not the inch, foot and yard. He looked closer at metric units of area and the same patterns emerged. The hectare is made up of 10,000 square metres or 100 ares, each being 10 x 10 metres. In Megalithic terms these could be seen as:

1 are   = 2 x 2 Megalithic Rods (12 x 12 MY)

1 hectare = 100 units of 2 x 2 Megalithic Rods

1 hectare = 1 kilometre x 2 Megalithic Rods

Studying other obsolete units proved to be very interesting. The old Irish acre of 7,840 square yards is a strange measure of land that turns out to be 40 Megalithic Yards x 40 Megalithic Rods to an accuracy greater that 99 percent. Next, the old Scottish acre of 6,150.4 square yards appeared particularly bizarre until Chris considered it in Megalithic terms and found that it is actually 75 Megalithic Yards x

100 Megalithic Yards to an accuracy greater than 99.6 percent.

Was the Megalithic Yard really the underlying key to a lost reality behind the modern measurement systems – both imperial and metric? We got together to digest this new information and asked ourselves whether there was a possibility we were beginning to see patterns that were not really there. The next procedure was to assess whether the relationships we had found using the assumed Megalithic Rod were really as remarkable as they seemed. The starting point had been to consider whether the rod of $16^1/_2$ feet (198 inches) had originally been defined as six Megalithic Yards. We then noticed that the metre also fits into the pattern. We looked again at all three potential versions of the rod in metric terms:

imperial rod	= $16^1/_2$ feet	= 5,029 millimetres
		(100 percent)
metric rod	= 5 metres	= 5,000 millimetres
		(99.42 percent)
Megalithic Rod	= 6 Megalithic Yards	= 4,978 millimetres
		(98.99 percent)

They were close – very close – but any observer could be forgiven for dismissing them as a coincidental fit. The way that the assumed Rod made sense of so many old units such as the Irish and Scottish acres was enough to stop us throwing away the notion. But for the moment, we could only view these observations as being of potential interest if future findings were to lend them further support. If not, even at this stage we were quite prepared to dismiss the whole idea.

We remained somewhat sceptical about the validity of the Megalithic Rod but we now had no doubts regarding the Megalithic weights and measures we had recreated. Perhaps the best way forward would be to look at another, better-understood culture, to ascertain whether Megalithic techniques were being used elsewhere in the world, either at the same time as the western European farmers, or more recently.

CONCLUSIONS

◎ A cube with sides of one-tenth of a Megalithic Yard holds one imperial pint of water and one imperial pound of grain to a very high level of accuracy. Doubling the length of the sides produces a capacity of one imperial gallon and doubling again produces a weight of one dry bushel.

◎ Spheres with diameters of six Megalithic Inches hold a litre and weigh a kilo, while a sphere that measures one and a half Megalithic Yards across holds one cubic metre of water and weighs a metric tonne. It seems, at first view, that the imperial and metric correspondence must be coincidence because both systems are relatively recent conventions.

◎ Investigation into the old unit of length known as the rod shows that it is extremely close to being equal to 5 metres and 6 Megalithic Yards. As such it appears to unite the two systems across all units of length and area, even making sense of peculiar, obsolete units such as the Irish and Scottish areas.

◎ The mathematics are easy to check and the pattern that emerges is powerful and simple yet, according to standard histories, it should not exist. All of this may be a coincidence of an unbelievably huge kind but we were not prepared to make that assumption at that stage.

CHAPTER 4

Sumerian Degrees

We had detected a very surprising system of weights and measures that stemmed directly and logically from the Megalithic Yard and could have been in use in and around the British Isles during the late Stone Age. This hypothetical system uses a common-sense approach and very simple technology. If these units were known to the Megalithic builders it means that pounds and pints were known and in use 5,000 years ago. Of course, we can never know for certain whether these units existed because the Megalithic people had no writing. However, it would have been very strange for a group of people to have used very accurate units of length for over 1,000 years and never to have adapted such units to establish weight and volume.

Without a means of gauging weight and volume, trade remains at a bartering level where each transaction has to be assessed by visual evaluation alone. The ability to identify a known quantity makes buying and selling a much more scientific process since it can be accurately repeated time after time. Using mutually accepted units of weight meant deals could be done at long range because it would be unnecessary to see the merchandise first to assess its quantity. For example, two pounds of deer meat can be agreed to have a value of one pint of beer.

Information is power, and it rarely just disappears. Indeed, the fact that the Megalithic units have an almost perfect relationship with modern measurements strongly suggests that there has been a continuity of this knowledge across the Great Wall of History. We therefore decided to bring our investigation back across that wall, to the first major civilization, to establish whether we could detect any connection with the Megalithic way of thinking. That brought us to the inventors of writing and the first known nation of international traders, the Sumerians, who lived in a number of powerful and historically important city states.

The Sumerian civilization

The region occupied by the Sumerians was between the Tigress and Euphrates rivers in what is now Iraq/Kuwait and, until recently, has always been known as Mesopotamia. Prehistoric peoples known as the Ubaidians had originally settled in the area establishing settlements that gradually developed into the important Sumerian cities of Adab, Eridu, Isin, Kish, Kullab, Lagash, Larsa, Nippur and Ur. As the land prospered, Semites from the Syrian and Arabian deserts moved in, both as peaceful immigrants and as raiders. Then circa 3250 BC the Sumerians arrived and began to intermarry with the native population. These small, dark-haired newcomers were intellectually and technologically sophisticated and spoke an agglutinative language that is unrelated to any other known language. (Agglutinative languages contain words formed through the combination of smaller morphemes [units that cannot be further divided] to express compound thoughts.)

As the Sumerians gained control the country grew rich and powerful, and art and architecture, as well as religious and ethical thought, flourished. The Sumerian language was adopted by those in the region and even in other lands it was considered the language of the intellectual. The cuneiform system of writing that the Sumerians invented evolved into the basic means of written communication used throughout the Middle East for the next 2,000 years. It is also believed that the Sumerians invented the wheel.

The first recorded ruler of Sumer was Etana, King of Kish, who reigned in approximately 2800 BC. The various city states frequently fought among themselves and by the 23rd century BC the power of the Sumerians had declined to such an extent that they could no longer defend themselves against foreign invasion. The Semitic ruler Sargon the Great conquered the entire area and founded a new capital at Agade, in northernmost Sumer, which became the wealthiest and most powerful city in the world. The indigenous people of northern Sumer and their conquerors gradually merged to become an ethnic and linguistic group known as the Akkadians.

The Akkadian dynasty lasted about a century, after which a people from the Zagros Mountains known as the Gutians sacked the city of Agade and eventually laid waste to the whole of Sumer. After several generations the Sumerians finally threw off the Gutian yoke, and the once-important city of Lagash again achieved prominence during the reign of Gudea, between 2144–2124 BC. Gudea was an extraordinarily pious and capable governor who left numerous statues of himself that still survive.

The Babylonian civilization

From about 2000 BC there was a slow change of phase that saw the decline of the Sumerian culture and the rise of what is called the Babylonian civilization, which flourished until the 6th century BC. The Babylonians modified and transformed their Sumerian heritage to suit their own culture and ethos, resulting in a way of life that was so efficient that it underwent relatively little change for about 1,200 years.

The area called Mesopotamia by the Greeks is known as 'the cradle of civilization' and was home to the Sumerian, Babylonian, Assyrian, and Chaldean cultures across thousands of years. It is difficult to isolate which achievements were made by each group because there was a continuous stream of development, particularly between the Sumerian and the Babylonian cultures. In many respects it is unnecessary to attempt to put clear divisions between these civilizations because they represent an evolution of the same mind-set.

Base 10 and base 60

The Sumerians are attributed with the development of mathematics. They used a combination of the base 10 and base 60 (sexagesimal) systems of counting as opposed to the simple base 10 or decimal system we use today. We are accustomed to thinking of 60 seconds to a minute and 60 minutes to an hour because our system of time derives from that of the Sumerians/Babylonians. By general consensus, the Sumerians are also attributed with inventing the idea of having a 360-degree circle, with each degree being subdivided into 60 minutes and each minute into 60 seconds.

Our first thought at this point was of how similar the breakdown of the circle was between the Megalithic 366 degrees and the Sumerian 360 degrees. We wondered whether the Sumerians originally used the 366-degree system but made a small downward adjustment when they invented their base 60 arithmetic. After all, being able to divide the circle into 6 lots of 60 must have been much more useful to them. However, we soon found that there was much more to it that a simple rounding down of someone else's system.

We had to remember that the number 360 was already important to the Megalithic builders because they had '6 lots of 60' in their Earth-related geometry, in which 366 degrees was subdivided into 60 minutes and then into 6 seconds. This had been the method that had produced a second of arc of the polar equator that was 366 Megalithic Yards in length, which was also equal to precisely 1,000 Minoan feet. So, we already had some sense of continuity between the Megalithic people of Britain and the Sumerians, who existed at about the same period but were thousands of miles distant from each other.

Barley seed

The next logical step was to look into what is known of Sumerian units of measurement, beginning with length. Today we have hundreds of different units for all kinds of specialized purposes, and the Sumerians were not so different to ourselves. Also, as with our civilization, units changed over hundreds of years but despite these complications there was always one unit that was central to a culture in the same way that the metre is to Europe and the foot is to the United States. The Mesopotamian cultures used a range of linear measurements at various times, depending on the item being measured, but there is a general consensus that a linear unit known as the 'kush' or 'barley cubit' was the main unit of length during Sumerian times.

The kush was made up of 180 'se' (believed to be pronounced something like 'shay') meaning 'barley seed'. Six se equalled one 'shu-si', or hand, and 30 shu-si equalled one kush. It is known that the kush was very close to half a metre in length and there is now an almost exact definition of their kush, thanks to two of the statues of the Sumerian King Gudea, mentioned above. A number of diorite statues were unearthed in Mesopotamia by Ernest de Sarzec in 1880 and two of these statues show King Gudea in a seated position with a tablet on his lap inscribed with plans for a temple. Along the side of the statue, opposite the figure, is a graduated rule, carefully executed and clearly intended to be a half-kush. The length of this first-hand example of a Sumerian half-kush has been gauged to be approximately 24.97 centimetres, which would mean the Sumerian kush was equivalent to 49.94 centimetres and the often used double-kush, which Professor Livio Stecchini believed should be 99.88 centimetres.[1]

Unfortunately, we do not have a finely-honed definition of the double kush because there are not enough samples available (compared to Thom's work or even that of Professor Graham) to extract one. We therefore took Professor Stecchini's value as possibly the best estimate that exists. However, we can be certain that the double-kush was remarkably close to being a modern metre and, while we might once have ignored this as a coincidence, we were now open to considering that there just might be a connection.

The fact that the kush was composed of 180 se, or barley seeds, was of immediate interest, bearing in mind our discoveries about grain and the avoirdupois pound. This also meant that there were 360 se in the double-kush, which was virtually a metre. We asked an expert (see p. 243–244) if there was any available information regarding the smallest unit of Sumerian linear measurement. The expert, a professor of mathematics, told us that 'the barley seed referred to as a se was not to be taken as a genuine barley seed because it was merely a convenient terminology used by the Sumerian scribes'. He went on to suggest that genuine barley seeds would be a fairly useless basis for any measuring system. We decided to see if this was the case. As far as we could ascertain, the barley seed has not changed a great deal since ancient Mesopotamian times, so we stuck a number of barley seeds together in rows, on adhesive tape, to see what they would measure. With the seeds

[1] Stecchini, L. C.: www.metrum.org/measures/index.htm

end to end, there are certainly far fewer than 180 barley seeds to a barley cubit. However, when they are arranged side by side (*see Colour Plate section*) they measure exactly what the se is supposed to measure, 180 barley seeds (on average) to the kush. We mention this little exercise to demonstrate the folly of failing to take the words of our ancient ancestors seriously. These people most certainly would not have referred to a barley seed if they had been talking about something completely different. (See Appendix 6 for more information on our experiments with barley seeds.) This also meant that there were 360 se (barley seeds) in a double-kush and, if the double-kush were turned into a circle, each se would therefore be equal to one degree.

The Sumerians had been familiar not only with the kush or barley cubit, but had also regularly used the half-kush (as depicted on the Gudea statues) and the double-kush – just as the Megalithic builders had regularly used half, whole and double Megalithic Yards in their constructions.

It is standard practice to assume that all units of length used prior to the metric system were approximate measures based on body parts, and the cubit is often said to have been the length from the elbow to the tip of the middle finger. While this may have been used as a market trader's rough measure it seemed patently absurd to believe that such a consistently accurate unit was derived from anyone's body parts. Such an idea is an insult to a people who were obviously highly talented and intelligent individuals. The question then arose: 'What was the origin of the half, full and double-kush?'

The Venus technique

Having already identified a foolproof process underpinning the Megalithic Yard, the natural starting point was to consider the Venus method. It is known that the Sumerians were great astronomers and they certainly invented geometry (attested to by the mathematical problems written into hundreds of clay tablets from the period), so they certainly had the ability to use the Venus technique. Again, we were in the happy position of being able to reverse-engineer the process. We could start with the supposed length of the half-kush from the Gudea statue for our hypothetical pendulum and work backwards to find out the possible equation that would have produced the desired result. First we needed to know at what rate a half-kush pendulum would beat and, by now we were very familiar with the formula for arriving at the period of time taken for any pendulum of a given length to swing. Alan looked at the half-kush, ran the pendulum formula through his calculator, then did it again before picking up the phone to Chris:

> 'I've just checked out the swing of a half-kush pendulum,' Alan announced without any preamble when Chris picked up the phone.

> 'Is it interesting?' Chris enquired.

> 'Interesting? You want interesting – I'll give you something interesting alright.'

> 'Go on then,' said Chris.

> 'One second! The pendulum period is one second!' he shouted triumphantly. 'Assuming that Stecchini's length of 99.88 is bang on, the time interval is actually 1.003 seconds, which is pretty damn close, don't you think.'

> 'Wow!' Chris replied. 'The Sumerians invented the second of time, and it now seems we may have uncovered the way they did it.'

To come out with a figure $3/1,000$ away from a modern second seemed much more than a mere coincidence. The double-kush of 99.88 centimetres also returned exactly the same near-perfect fit, though in this case for one beat of the pendulum. (The *period* of a pendulum is the swing from one side to the other and back again, whereas the *beat* is the single movement from one side to the other.)

We felt justified in rejecting any notion that these Sumerian primary units of length coincidentally produced such a good fit to the Sumerian-devised second of time when used as a pendulum. It looked as though the kush and the second were two halves of the same phenomenon: the time period and length that were brought together by the acceleration (due to gravity) of the Earth at the latitude of Sumer. This realization is of great significance. Modern physics accepts that time and space (meaning linear distance) can be seen as different expressions of the same thing, which both the Megalithic peoples and the Sumerians seem to have known, at least at a mathematical level.

It did indeed seem that the Sumerians must have used the Megalithic technique of measuring the spin of the Earth by tracking and timing Venus. The question was: 'What part of a circle was used and how many beats were counted?' This should be easy to work out because we knew a great deal more about the inhabitants of the land of Sumer than we do about those of the British Isles at that time. We started with the logical assumption that they would have used one Sumerian/Babylonian degree and therefore $1/360$ part of a circle – just as we would today. It was then a straightforward calculation to establish that the double-kush pendulum would achieve 120 periods or 240 beats in the time it took Venus to move through one degree. Therefore, a Sumerian builder could check his half-kush or double-kush employing exactly the same methodology as the Megalithic builder, though inputting the numbers that were important to his own civilization. The result was to define the second of time that is incredibly close to the one that we still use today, producing a result that was to all intents and purpose, the same as the metre.

The numbers were once again too neat to be a random event. This experiment using the half-kush and one degree of the Sumerian circle could easily have produced in any odd number. However, this was not the case, and the result clearly showed that the originators of the system had employed the Sumerian base number of 60. This was evident because 120 is twice 60 and 240 is 4 times 60. Added together they produce 360 – the number of degrees in a circle.

While this calculation made perfect sense to us, we needed to know if there was any record of the Sumerians/Babylonians using a period of time equal to 240 seconds as marked out by 240 beats of a double-kush pendulum. We soon found that their basic division of a day was known as a 'gesh' and – amazingly – it was 240 seconds in length! Everything fitted like a beautiful jigsaw puzzle!

We had earlier used Thom's technique of reverse-engineering to work out the Venus and pendulum techniques used by the Megalithic people, though of course in the absence of written records from this period and geographical location, we could not know whether the period of time during which their pendulum swung had been given a name. But the Sumerians *had* kept records – the gesh – and remarkably they had a name for precisely the period of time we had deduced as being necessary for the method of making a half-kush and a double-kush – the gesh. There could be no doubt – like the Megalithic peoples the Sumerians had used the Venus pendulum method!

Venus is known to have a very special place in Sumerian culture. The planet was first known to the astronomer-priests or 'baru' as 'Inanna', which meant 'Queen of Heaven'. Later, Venus was also known as 'Ishtar'. Here was further evidence to support our original hypothesis of the Megalithic technique. Having applied a methodology from Megalithic Britain we had arrived at a matrix that interweaves the second of time, the Sumerian kush, the Sumerian base 60 system, the Sumerian 360-degree circle and the gesh (the basic Sumerian division of the day). The chances of all this happening with such perfection are as close to zero as anything could ever be!

The Sumerian calendar

The existence of the second and the gesh of 240 seconds made us think more closely about the whole structure of Sumerian timekeeping. All experts are agreed that the Sumerians invented the 360-degree circle, which matched the number of days in their ritual year. The Sumerian calendar is known to be lunar in origin and had probably sprung from roots so old they are lost to us completely. But we can be sure that the astronomer-priests of Sumer knew perfectly well that there was a significant discrepancy between 12 lunar months of just over $29^1/_2$ days and the true solar year of $365^1/_4$ days.

The most important festival for the Sumerians was the barley festival, at which time Christians now celebrate Easter. Then, as now, it was symbolic of death and resurrection and it was calculated in the same way as Easter – as the first full Moon after the vernal equinox (one of only two times a year that the Sun rises due east and sets due west, and the day and night are of equal length) which falls on or around 21st March. The Sumerians called this festival 'Barag-Zag-Gar', and it represented the start of their year. The 12 months were then counted off into lunar months, rounded up to 30 days each, giving them a 360-day year. The problem of the difference between the 360-day year and the true solar year of 365 days was solved by allowing the spare days to accumulate until there were enough of them to add an intercalary month to the calendar. This extra month the Sumerians called 'Itu-diri'. This procedure ensured that the first full Moon after the barley harvest was that of Barag-Zag-Gar, as it should be, and the balance between solar and lunar years was periodically restored.

Just as the Sumerians had 360 days in a year, they split each day into 360 units known as 'gesh'. Contemporary records show that the Sumerian astronomer-priests originally had 12 rather than 24 hours in a day. They did this primarily because they loved 'wheels within wheels' and they saw the day as a microcosm of the year – as there were 12 months in the year there should be 12 hours in a day. A further reason relates to the zodiac.

The Sun, Moon and all the planets of our solar system, when viewed from Earth, keep to the same path across the heavens known as the 'plane of the ecliptic'. From an unknown time in distant prehistory this band of the heavens has been split into 12 sections associated with zodiac signs. Each section is named after groups of stars within it, which have been interpreted as patterns that became memorable to the stargazers over countless generations. The Sumerians, who used the concept of the zodiac, were great Moon watchers. They observed the Earth's companion planet passing month by month from one zodiac sign to the next, with full Moons occurring in successive zodiac signs. In addition, they would have been aware that the Sun appears to move from one zodiac sign to the next during the period of a month. These same zodiac signs passed over their heads each day as the Earth turned on its axis between one sunrise and the next. Since Sumerians split the year into 360 days and the day into 360 gesh as well as dividing the day and the year into 12 equal units, it follows that there were 30 gesh during each zodiac sign.

The Sumerians were aware that the seasons moved through the full zodiac once each year and the zodiac moved overhead once each day. So here again was a potentially deliberate 'wheel within a wheel' effect

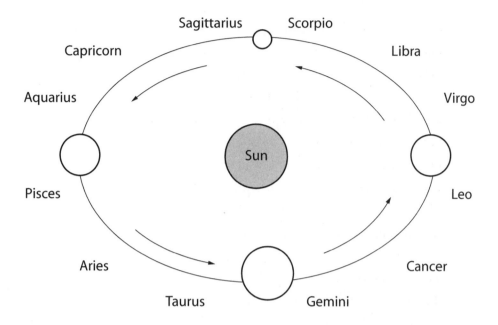

The Earth revolves around the Sun once per year. The background stars are effectively stationary and the Sun appears to move by one Megalithic Degree relative to them. After one year the stars will appear to have returned to their starting positions.

because they had adopted the following pattern:

year = 12 months each made up of 30 days

day = 12 hours each made up of 30 gesh

Our next step was to look at the behaviour of the Moon because it occurred to us that these gesh might also have been considered to be a lunar phenomenon. We know from historical records that the Sumerians judged the period from one full Moon to the next as being 30 days, which is not too far away from its exact period of 29.53059 days and is, in any case, the nearest integer number available. So, here was another 'wheel within a wheel'.

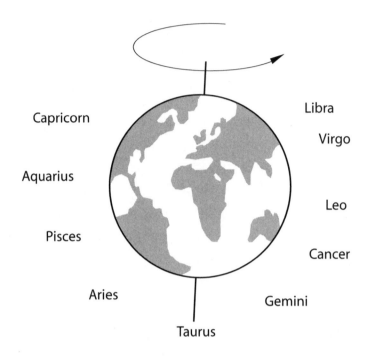

The turning Earth and the zodiac.

year	=	360 days
month	=	360 hours
day	=	360 gesh

Each of the Sumerian hours represented one degree of the Moon's journey around the Earth and every degree of the Moon's journey was split again, by 60, to give minutes of arc and by 60 again to give seconds of arc.

After ten years of research, the answer came to us in a flash. Minutes and seconds of time in the Sumerian 12-hour day were Moon minutes and Moon seconds of arc. We still employ them today, with one exception. The Sumerians are known to have used halves and doubles of all their measuring units and for different mathematical purposes. The astronomer-priests also considered a day to be composed of 12 'double' hours, which ultimately became 24 hours in the Babylonian system. The Egyptians also used a 24-hour day, which is the route by which the 24 hours has passed down to our own times. When the length of the hour was halved, knowledge of the minutes and seconds remained and because there had to be 60 minutes to an hour, these units were also halved.

The Sumerian minutes and seconds of time were originally twice the length of the ones we use today but we can now see that there was a real concept behind the second of time: the purpose of the second was to turn sky time into linear length!

The full Sumerian time system is utterly sensational! Not only is it based on the Sun and the stars of the zodiac, it also takes in the cycles of the Moon.

In an integer sense, the Moon takes 30 days to complete its circle around the Earth. That circle is split into 360 units, which are hours. Each of these hours is split by 60 and 60 again to create seconds of time. All of this fits with everything we know about number usage. The main difference between the Sumerian system and our present decimal system is that the Sumerians used a 60 and 10 base combined, whereas the decimal system employs a 10 base in all cases. The Sumerians recognized that 360 is a very useful number, since it is divisible by so many other numbers. Most importantly it equals 6 x 10 x 6. As a result the Sumerian priests used a counting system that alternated between multiples of 6 and 10 with symbols as shown below:

Sumerian symbols.

Ten small wedges equalled 1 small circle, 6 small circles equalled one large wedge, 10 large wedges equalled 1 large circle, and so on. The numbers worked as follows:

Step	Multiple		Value
1.	1	=	1
2.	x 10	=	10
3.	x 6	=	60
4.	x 10	=	600
5.	x 6	=	3,600
6.	x 10	=	36,000
7.	x 6	=	216,000
8.	x 10	=	2,160,000
9.	x 6	=	12,960,000
10.	x 10	=	129,600,000

Religious connotations

It is surely the case that there was also a deeply religious aspect to both the numbers and the phenomena they measured. Even the second of time (related as the Sumerians believed it to be to the Moon) probably had a 'mystical' feel when associated with the magic of the double-kush pendulum. We can get some idea of this when we look at Sumerian mythology. We have already observed that the first and therefore the most important month of the year was known by the Sumerians as Barag-Zag-Gar. This month commenced on the day of the first full Moon, after the barley harvest. This period of the year could have been sacred to only one deity. Her name was 'Nisaba', one of the most important deities in the Sumerian pantheon, and a goddess with very special responsibilities. Nisaba was, first and foremost, the barley goddess. We were intrigued to discover, however, that among her many attributes she was said to be the goddess responsible for:

'The measuring lines to measure the heavens.'[2]

As we looked more closely at the humble barley seed we were soon to find that it held spectacular properties for the Sumerians. Having looked at the Sumerian civilization in the light of the principles used by the Megalithic builders we could see a clear pattern to their units of length and those of time. We now needed to look at their units of weight and capacity.

Weight and capacity

When we had deduced possible units of weight and capacity from Megalithic units of length, they had turned out to be the same as modern imperial units. Now we needed to apply the same logic to the Sumerian situation. Because the double-kush was so close to the metre, we did not need a calculator to tell us that if the Sumerians had followed the same route of making a cube with sides one tenth of a double-cubit, they must have been using units almost identical to the kilogram and the litre for weight and volume.

Unlike the Megalithic situation, contemporary records of Sumerian weights and measures still exist, so all we had to do was to look up the units that are known to have been used some 4,000 years ago in Mesopotamia. Despite our previous discoveries, we were nevertheless stunned to learn that the Sumerians/Babylonians had indeed used units that were effectively the half-kilogram and the litre! The Sumerian unit of mass, the 'mana', is consistently described by archaeologists as being 'about half a kilogram', while the 'sila', the basic unit of volume, has been shown to be very close to a litre.

The double-kush is said to be something very close to 99.88

2 Fryman-Kensky: *In the Wake of the Goddesses*. Fawcet Columbine, New York, 1992.

centimetres in length, so a cube with sides of one-tenth of this would have sides of 9.988 centimetres. The volume of water that such a cube could hold would be 996.4 centilitres, less than 4 centilitres short of a litre of 1,000 centilitres, The sila is therefore equal to the amount of water that would fit into a one-tenth double-kush cube. The weight of the water in such a cube should represent the standard unit of mass. However, the mana weighs around half a kilogram, whereas it is clear that the true weight of one litre of water should be a full kilogram. The Sumerians, like the Megalithic people, regularly used halves and doubles of principal units and we wonder whether the Sumerian texts have been slightly misinterpreted and a mana did originally weigh a kilogram or, more likely, that the Sumerians found this unit cumbersome and so halved it for most day-to-day purposes.

We found that we were not the first researchers to suggest that the Sumerians used cubes to turn linear length into mass and volume. The late Professor of the History of Science, Livio C. Stecchini, remained convinced all his life that it was obvious that theoretical cubes had been used by the Sumerians to create mass and volume measures from the kush and double-kush. Present orthodoxy disagrees with this premise, preferring to believe that these mass and volume weights were somehow tortuously derived from Sumerian units of area. The general argument against Stecchini's idea is based upon the fact that no cubes of the right size have ever been found in Sumer. The learned professor dismissed this observation by noting that in the case of the metric system, 'original units for cubing one-tenth of a metre were, and still are, cylinders and not cubes'. In any case, even if the cubes had existed, they would have been very few in number and cannot reasonably be expected to automatically turn up in the archaeological record.

Our research has shown that the Megalithic people of the area around the British Isles used a unit of length that implies that they could have and probably did use the equivalent of the imperial pound and pint. Now, using the same model we had discovered that the people of ancient Mesopotamia used units of length, weight and capacity that have a remarkable correspondence to the metric system. How could this be?

The recorded origins of the units within the imperial system are just about impossible to trace but the metric system was designed 'from the ground up' by a team of scientists working in France during the late 18th century. The chances of the pound and the pint surviving for thousands of years seem remote, but did the French deliberately copy the Sumerian units?

	Degrees to circle	Minutes to a degree	Seconds to a minute	Venus period	Beats counted	Pendulum length
Megalithic	366	60	6	236 seconds	366	$1/_2$ Megalithic Yard
Sumerian	360	60	60	240 seconds (1 gesh)	240 (one per second)	1 Double-Kush (360 se)

	Division of pendulum used for sides of a cube		Capacity of cube	Weight of cube
Megalithic	(One tenth of double length) 4 Megalithic Inches		1 imperial pint (water-filled)	1 imperial pound (grain-filled)
Sumerian	(One tenth) 36 se		1 Litre (water-filled)	1 Kilo (water-filled)

Comparison of the Megalithic and Sumerian systems of geometry and the consequences for weight and capacity units.

Conclusions

◎ The Sumerians/Babylonians used a system of mathematics that used base 60, which is the reason why we still have 60 seconds to the minute and 60 minutes to the hour. They also invented the 360-degree circle, which was also subdivided into minutes and seconds. In addition, they used a standard unit of length that is believed to be 99.88 centimetres – almost exactly equivalent to the modern metre.

◎ The Sumerians'/Babylonians' double-kush of 99.88 centimetres was reproduced by means of swinging a pendulum with a beat of one second 240 times to define a unit of time they called a 'gesh'.

◎ The Sumerians/Babylonians also developed an elaborate system of ritual timekeeping based on the movements of the Moon with 360 days per year, 360 hours per month and 360 gesh (240 seconds) per day.

◎ From their unit of length the Sumerians derived units of weight and capacity that are incredibly close to the kilo and the litre. To all intents and purposes it is fair to say that the metric system was in use more than 3,000 years before the French invented it.

CHAPTER 5

The Rebirth of the Metric System

The age of great Megalithic building began before 3000 BC and many of the major sites had been abandoned by the middle of the 3rd century BC. The last remnants of the Megalithic builders seem to have disappeared by about 1500 BC, which means that they certainly overlapped with the Minoan culture that clearly used the same 366 method of geometry. From the Iron Age until the rise of the Roman Empire, much of what is now the British Isles and France was inhabited by the Celts. There is no record of whether the Celts inherited any of the weights and measures that had been used by the Megalithic builders but it is not unreasonable to consider that the old units may have survived in an original or in a modified form.

French weights and measures

Only with the spread of the Roman Empire did these far western regions of Europe gain a recognizable uniformity in terms of weights and measures. Rome held sway over Gaul (France) and Britain until the beginning of the 6th century AD when the Roman legions were recalled and the area fell into that historically murky period known as the 'Dark Ages'. The withdrawal of the legions led to a power vacuum in both Britain and Gaul which, through the peculiar set of circumstances prevailing, gave way to feudalism, a system under which international trade was not especially desired or encouraged. However, if any country was going to prosper and grow strong, a degree of cross-border cooperation was inevitable. The process was helped somewhat by the development of important sites of commerce, particularly in the area of northern France which eventually became known as Champagne.

In the 12th and 13th centuries the Champagne fairs, held regularly in specific towns and cities in the region, positively encouraged merchants from all over Europe and beyond to exchange goods. These were huge trade fairs (rather than markets for consumers) that were held under the authority of the dukes of Champagne and new, or apparently new weights and measures appeared at this time. Many British people will be surprised to learn that their much-loved pound and ounce made their first known appearance as French units at these fairs.

It is certain that both units of length and weight were created deliberately to serve the fairs in an attempt to offer common measures that everyone could understand and use without confusion. With the gradual demise in the importance of the fairs and with so much fighting taking place between the emerging nation states of the region, units of length and weight often became a strictly local matter, though frequently with underlying aspects of the old Roman system. Britain struggled but somehow managed with a seemingly incomprehensible muddle of different units, though the country we now know as France

THE REBIRTH OF THE METRIC SYSTEM

was in an even worse state.

Prior to the early 14th century, France was a series of different states which had not been united since Roman times. These were only welded together again as a result of conquests and dynastic unions resulting in virtual chaos, with a wealth of different length, weight and volume unit names and sizes existing simultaneously across the new country. Matters were made even more complicated by the fact that some units retained a common name in different regions even though they differed in size. The chaos continued until some new data on the circumference of the Earth was published in 1670 by Jean Picard, a priest and an astronomer living in La Flèche. Picard accurately assessed the polar circumference of the Earth using the distance from Sourdon near Amiens, to Malvoisine south of Paris, as his test area. This gave another priest an inspired thought.

A new system

Father Gabriel Mouton of St Paul's Church in Lyon put forward the suggestion that France should design a completely original set of decimalized weights and measures based upon an agreed fraction of the length of one minute of arc of the newly-measured polar circumference of the planet. The idea immediately caught the imagination of leading thinkers, but Picard did not agree with Mouton's suggestion for the means of devising a new linear measure. Instead, together with astronomer Ole Römer (a distinguished scientist from Copenhagen who spent long periods in France and Germany), Picard proposed that the new unit of linear length upon which everything else could be based, should be precisely the length of a pendulum with a beat of one second of time.

The 'seconds pendulum'

The concept of a 'seconds pendulum' had been first identified by Galileo earlier in the same century when he became the first recorded European to actively experiment with pendulums, though it was left to the Englishman Isaac Newton (1643–1727) to later establish correct dimensions for the seconds pendulum. The device had a particular fascination for Newton, who experimented extensively in all matters pertaining to gravity. Newton had calculated that a freely-swinging pendulum, at a location of 45 degrees latitude, with a beat of exactly 1 second, would measure 39.14912 inches in length which was correct to within one twenty-five thousandth of a second. (While this is all of great historical interest we demonstrated in the last chapter that the Sumerians had achieved all these objectives some 3,500 years earlier.)

It was known by the time of Picard and Römer that gravity did not act equally on all parts of the planet because the Earth is an oblique spheroid rather than a perfect sphere. The astronomers seem to have favoured basing the new linear unit on the seconds pendulum measured at Paris, though Newton's 45-degree latitude was also considered, as was a seconds pendulum set for the equator.

Despite the debates about the best way forward nothing further seems to have happened regarding the new French system until the 14th July 1789 when the Bastille was stormed, igniting a revolution that was to change that country for ever. The problem of the disparate weights and measures had been tolerated because there were always greater problems to be confronted but after the revolution, with the beginning of a completely new regime, the populace could be persuaded to change everything it had known for generations in terms of weights and measures.

Only a year after the start of the French Revolution, in 1790, the Constituent Assembly of France was on the receiving end of a report from Charles-Maurice Talleyrand Perigord, Bishop of Autun. Talleyrand was a larger-than-life character and certainly no scientist, yet he resurrected the proposition of a new system of weights and measures, based on a standard to be derived from the length of a pendulum at 45 degrees north (45 degrees being exactly halfway between the equator and the poles.)

The reason for Talleyrand's interference in such matters probably stemmed from his success as a diplomat. At almost exactly the same time as revolutionary France was thinking in terms of a new measuring system, across the Channel in England scientific minds were also turning in the same direction. Talleyrand desperately wanted to achieve a lasting peace between France and Britain, an heroic effort that was doomed to failure. It is also known that he had friends within the British Royal Society as well as in London-based masonic lodges. He went so far as to suggest collaboration between the Académie des Sciences in Paris and the Royal Society of London in order to try and establish the length of a seconds pendulum to the very highest level of accuracy. At the time, Louis XVI was still clinging to the French throne and the Assembly passed a decree asking Louis to write to the British king, George III. The letter was to suggest that:

> 'Parliament should meet with the National Assembly for the fixation of national units of weights and measures so that com-missioners of the French Academy could meet with an equal number from the Royal Society in the most convenient place to determine at 45° latitude or at any other preferred latitude the length of the [*seconds*] pendulum and produce an invariable model for all weights and measures.'

It is unlikely that the request of the French Assembly was ever acted upon by Louis because no trace of such a letter exists in British archives.

Louis was a worried man and doubtless thought that to force an entirely new measuring system on a country already so troubled might be the last straw. Almost in tandem with the suggested letter to Britain, the Assembly set up a commission to look into a new metric system. It was composed of five brilliant scientists and mathematicians. These men were Laplace, Lagrange, Monge, Borda and Condorcet. The report produced by this commission was presented to the French Academy on 19th March 1791.

It was at this time that the concept of the seconds pendulum was more or less abandoned as the preferred unit for the new linear measurement because it was reluctantly decided that no timepiece existed that could accurately measure one second of time. The commission was left with no option but to return to Father Mouton's original suggestion that the new unit should be derived from an extremely accurate assessment of the distance between the North Pole and the equator and to make the new linear unit a subdivision of this distance. Despite this decision, the seconds pendulum was far from forgotten. One of the commission's recommendations was:

'To make observations at latitude 45° for determining the number of vibrations in a day, and in a vacuum at sea level, of a simple pendulum equal in length when at the temperature of melting ice, to the ten-millionth part of the meridian quadrant with a view to the possibility of restoring the length of the new standard unit, at any future time, by pendulum observation.'

The subdivision of polar circumference

So the seconds pendulum was retained as a safety backup should the new unit of length ever be lost. This indicates that the French team had chosen a subdivision of polar circumference that was as close to the seconds pendulum as they could achieve using a very round number. They settled on one ten-millionth part of the meridian quadrant – which meant that the new unit was one forty-millionth part the of the polar circumference of the Earth. This unit was eventually to be named the 'metre'. It is clear from the wording of the report presented by the commission that it was aware of the very slight difference in length between the established seconds pendulum and the proposed linear unit.

The seconds pendulum was still not forgotten, even in the later stages of the drive towards the metric system. The report of the fieldwork was dated 30th April 1799. Among its observations as reported by R. D. Connor was this:

> 'The length of a seconds pendulum at Paris at 0° C in vacuum at sea level is 0.99385 metres'. (*This last is equivalent to a period of a pendulum of length 1m being 2.00618 seconds at Paris, latitude 48° 52.*)

The seconds pendulum corrected metre came into official existence on 10th December 1799. However, the metric system in its entirety did not become obligatory until 1st January 1840. It is surprising how many sources still quote the Emperor Napoleon as having instigated metrication, but nothing could be further from the truth. Napoleon disliked the entire metric system and he is reported to have said:

> 'I can understand $^1/_{12}$ of an inch but not $^1/_{1000}$ of a metre!'

Having set the length for the metre the commission identified their longest unit of length as the kilometre at 1,000 metres, and the shortest was the millimetre at $^1/_{1,000}$ of the metre. In between they added the centimetre, being ten times larger than a millimetre and 100 times smaller than the metre. Next they turned their attention to the basic units of capacity and mass, which they derived in the simplest manner possible. They took a length of one tenth of a metre (ten centimetres) and used it to dictate the sides of a cube. This cube was then filled with distilled water (under very strict temperature and pressure requirements) and the volume occupied by the water was called a litre, while its weight was designated the kilogram.

The 'metric' system

Suddenly the metric system had been resurrected. Because the inspiration for the metre had originally been the seconds pendulum and because the French scientists had followed the same logic as their Sumerian forebears, the double-kush was back under a new name!

It appears that none of these French scientists questioned what a second of time actually was or where it had come from, except that it represented $1/86,400$ part of a mean solar day. They knew it had originated from ancient Mesopotamia but the Sumerian culture had not been identified at the time. It was much later that archaeological digs in the sands of Mesopotamia began to turn up scores of cuneiform tablets and slowly some people began to notice the amazing similarities between the Sumerian measurement system and the metric system. Professor Stecchini has shown how there was distinct embarrassment in academic circles at the convergence of a new and scientifically-based system with that of the most ancient documented culture on the planet.

There was once a great deal of controversy regarding Mesopotamian linear lengths, weights and measures and their 'fit' with the metric system. It has now become standard academic form to deny that either the Sumerians or the Babylonians could, or would have wanted to, create cubes or one-tenth the double-kush, in order to produce a fully-integrated measuring system.

The facts are self-evident and the reason why the metric system is so similar to the Mesopotamian model is no puzzle. The metre was chosen on the grounds that it was a provable geophysical unit, adopted because it so closely approximated the seconds pendulum, which itself was captivating scientists from Newton's time onwards. Indeed, when the Imperial Weights and Measures Acts of the 19th century were passed in Britain, instructions were given that these too were to be checked against the seconds pendulum if the created units were ever lost or damaged.

The French team that did not trust their late 18th-century timepieces would no doubt be amazed to learn that one day their metre would be defined as the distance travelled by light in a vacuum in a time interval of $1/299,792,458$ second. We now have the science to measure such tiny events but it remains a fact that the true seconds pendulum lies behind this definition. Bearing in mind that a pendulum length changes somewhat according to the latitude at which it is checked, the astronomer-priests of old made an extremely good job not only of defining the second of time, but also of showing what it meant in linear terms. The double-kush pendulum ticks away seconds with an error of only one five-thousandth of a second, an error that to anyone except the most fastidious Grand Prix racing driver means nothing!

We had been more than perplexed when we discovered that spheres with diameters measured in Megalithic units produce volumes that conform to cubic metres, litres and metric tonnes. It had seemed ridiculous in the extreme – but now we could see an underlying pattern emerging. The use of the second and the pendulum had drawn the French team into the ancient matrix that held some deep reality from the turning of the Earth. We really needed to understand better what a second of time actually is, but first we decided to see if there were any other recent measurement systems that may provide an additional piece for our giant jigsaw puzzle.

CONCLUSIONS

◎ Following the French Revolution the Académie des Sciences
decided to introduce a new system of decimal weights and
measures that was to be based on the length derived from a
pendulum that produced a time interval of one second. Using
this ancient Mesopotamian measure of time would have
automatically reinvented the double-kush without the fact
being realized. Eventually they had to concede that their
timepieces were not accurate enough to measure a precise
second and they therefore used a subdivision of the globe from
the equator to the North Pole as the basis of the new metric
system. The metre that was settled upon was one 10,000,000th
part of the Earth's quadrant and extremely close in length to
the seconds pendulum that they had originally wanted to
achieve.

◎ The seconds pendulum was used as a backup means of
recreating the metre and even the imperial system used this
same technique for possible emergencies. Having reinvented
the double-kush the French then proceeded to reincarnate the
ancient Mesopotamian units of weight and capacity by means
of cubes that were on a one-tenth subdivision of the metre.
Professor Livio C. Stecchini has shown how there was a later
realization that this supposedly new, scientifically-based system
was virtually identical to the Mesopotamian one used several
thousand years before.

◎ We had still not explained why spheres with diameters of
Megalithic dimensions produce volumes from the metric
system – but we had established that the 'metric' system was far
from a recent invention as is generally claimed.

CHAPTER 6

The Jefferson Report

The social cauldron that was the French Revolution had given rise to the development of a scientific measuring system fit for an ambitious new republic. On the other side of the Atlantic another fledgling nation was steadily establishing itself after an eight-year war for independence that had finished in 1783. The American War of Independence had seen 13 British colonies on the eastern seaboard of North America reject their parent country of Great Britain to form the United States of America.

Thomas Jefferson

One of the architects of what is now the world's only superpower was Thomas Jefferson. This Virginian aristocrat was one of the most brilliant American exponents of the Enlightenment, a political philosophy that he applied to the task of nation-building. It was Jefferson who drafted the famous Declaration of Independence that was signed on 4th July 1776, in his capital city of Philadelphia.

The 4th July was to become a significant date in the life of this outstanding statesman. Not only was his Declaration of Independence signed on that day but he also died on 4th July 1826. Of special interest to us is the fact that Thomas Jefferson drafted a particularly significant document, once again on the 4th July – this time in the year 1790. [1]

Jefferson's decimal system

We had been looking for other modern systems of measurement and found that Thomas Jefferson had created his own version of a decimal system of weights and measures just ahead of the French. The report on the metric system, prepared by Pierre Simon Laplace and his colleagues, was presented to the Académie des Sciences on 19th March 1791, but Jefferson had submitted his report to the House of Representatives in Philadelphia more than nine months earlier.

Jefferson's revolutionary concept of unified decimal measures, weights and coins was brilliant but was never adopted, except for his currency idea, the dollar, which arrived two years later. It is certain that Jefferson knew about the events unfolding in France because he was the American representative in France between 1784 and 1789, before returning to the United States to become Secretary of State in George Washington's government. The document Jefferson submitted confirms his awareness of European ideas of the same ilk:

> '... a printed copy of a proposition made by the Bishop of Autun, to the National Assembly of France, on the subject of weights and measures; and three days afterwards I received, through the channel of the public papers, the speech of Sir John Riggs Miller, of April 13th, in the British House of Commons, on the same subject.'

Jefferson may have been influenced by the French idea of a national

[1] A full account of what Jefferson had to say can be found at http://www.yale.edu/lawweb/avalon/jeffplan.htm and on a number of other websites.

measurement system but it is clear from the nature of his recommendations that he had developed his methodology through a train of logic.

As we read his words we were gladdened to discover that this great
man had shared our own deductions regarding a starting point for any
standard linear length, more than two centuries before our time. His
opening words set out the fundamental truths as he saw them, which
confirmed all our own thoughts about the starting point for creating
any natural unit of measurement at all.

> 'There exists not in nature, as far as has been hitherto observed,
> a single subject or species of subject, accessible to man, which
> presents one constant and uniform dimension.'

Jefferson clearly stated his belief that nobody in known history had
ever identified a naturally-occurring object or event that provides a
repeatable unit of measurement. He then went on to clarify that there
is only one candidate. He came to the same conclusion we had:

> 'The globe of the earth itself, indeed, might be considered as
> invariable in all its dimensions, and that its circumference would
> furnish an invariable measure; but no one of its circles, great or
> small, is accessible to measurement through all its parts, and the
> various trials to measure definite portions of them, have been of
> such various results as to show there is no dependence on that
> operation for certainty.
>
> Matter, then, by its mere extension, furnishing nothing
> invariable, its motion is the only remaining resource.
>
> The motion of the earth round its axis, though not absolutely
> uniform and invariable, may be considered as such for every
> human purpose. It is measured obviously, but unequally, by the
> departure of a given meridian from the sun, and its return to it,

constituting a solar day. Throwing together the inequalities of solar days, a mean interval, or day, has been found, and divided, by very general consent, into 86,400 equal parts.'

Here Jefferson referred to the second of time, taking for granted that it is an accepted starting point. He therefore had no intention of changing the accepted method of measuring time. He then followed the exact process we had identified as being the principle used by the Stone Age Britons:

'A pendulum, vibrating freely, in small and equal arcs, may be so adjusted in its length, as, by its vibrations, to make this division of the earth's motion into 86,400 equal parts, called seconds of mean time.

Such a pendulum, then, becomes itself a measure of determinate length, to which all others may be referred to as a standard.'

Jefferson could not have known it, but here he was describing a process that had been used by humankind for more than 5,000 years. He next identified the characteristics of the pendulum technique:

'Both theory and experience prove that, to preserve its isochronism [uniformity in time], it must be shorter towards the equator, and longer towards the poles. The height of the situation above the common level, as being an increment to the radius of the earth, diminishes the length of the pendulum.'

Belonging to a mechanical age, Jefferson identified the potential for the engine that swings the pendulum to interfere in the process. However, if swung by hand there would be no such problem and we doubt that an engine would affect the pendulum length unless it was clumsily applied:

'To continue small and equal vibrations, through a sufficient length of time, and to count these vibrations, machinery and a power are necessary, which may exert a small but constant effort to renew the waste of motion; and the difficulty is so to apply these, as that they shall neither retard nor accelerate the vibrations.'

Jefferson's rod

He next put forward a suggestion for an improvement to the method using the latest technology available at the time:

'In order to avoid the uncertainties which respect the centre of oscillation, it has been proposed by Mr Leslie, an ingenious artist of Philadelphia, to substitute, for the pendulum, a uniform cylindrical rod, without a bob.

Could the diameter of such a rod be infinitely small, the centre of oscillation would be exactly at two-thirds of the whole length, measured from the point of suspension. Giving it a diameter which shall render it sufficiently inflexible, the centre will be displaced, indeed; but, in a second rod not the six hundred thousandth part of its length, and not the hundredth part as much as in a second pendulum with a spherical bob of proper diameter. This displacement is so infinitely minute, then, that we may consider the centre of oscillation, for all practical purposes, as residing at two-thirds of the length from the centre of suspension. The distance between these two centres might be easily and accurately ascertained in practice. But the whole rod is better for a standard than any portion of it, because sensibly defined at both its extremities.'

The 'rod' described by Mr Leslie is a ridged strip of metal without a weight on the end. This means that the weight of the rod itself responds to the Earth's gravity rather than the stone at the end of a piece of twine. It is more accurate than a pendulum but Jefferson pointed out that such a rod will always be 50 percent longer than a pendulum to produce the same time interval. As the seconds pendulum is a tiny fraction less than a metre, the rod described here is a fraction under 1.5 metres, at 149.158 centimetres. It is also almost exactly three Sumerian kush.

Next, Jefferson considered the effect of using the rod at different latitudes, which will result in small variations. He discussed using 45 degrees north because it is mid-way between the equator and the North Pole, but curiously he also chose 31 degrees north, which is a latitude than runs through the land that was ancient Sumer:

> 'The difference between the second rod for 45° of latitude, and that for 31°, our other extreme, is to be examined.
>
> The second pendulum for 45° of latitude, according to Sir Isaac Newton's computation, must be of 39.14912 inches English measure; and a rod, to vibrate in the same time, must be of the same length between the centres of suspension and oscillation; and, consequently, its whole length 58.7 (or, more exactly, 58.72368) inches. This is longer than the rod which shall vibrate seconds in the 31° of latitude, by about $1/679$ part of its whole length; a difference so minute, that it might be neglected, as insensible, for the common purposes of life, but, in cases requiring perfect exactness, the second rod, found by trial of its vibrations in any part of the United States, may be corrected by computation for the latitude of the place, and so brought exactly to the standard of 45°.

By making the experiment in the level of the ocean, the difference will be avoided, which a higher position might occasion.'

Jefferson then makes his recommendation that the standard of measure of length should be derived from a uniform cylindrical rod of iron:

'...of such length as, in latitude 45°, in the level of the ocean, and in a cellar, or other place, the temperature of which does not vary throughout the year, shall perform its vibrations in small and equal arcs, in one second of mean time.'

The solution to all measurements

Having innocently adopted the Sumerian second as the unit of time, Jefferson's new unit had to be related to the Mesopotamian kush – and the Megalithic Yard. This he saw as the solution to all measurements including coinage, where each coin was simply a known weight of precious metal. He continued by saying:

'A standard of invariable length being thus obtained, we may proceed to identify, by that, the measures, weights and coins of the United States.'

At this point in his report, Jefferson referred to the origin of the weights and measures then currently in use in the United States. He wanted to better understand their origin:

'The first settlers of these States, having come chiefly from England, brought with them the measures and weights of that country. These alone are generally established among us, either by law or usage; and these, therefore, are alone to be retained and fixed. We must resort to that country for information of what they are, or ought to be.

This rests, principally, on the evidence of certain standard measures and weights, which have been preserved, of long time, in different deposits. But differences among these having been known to exist, the House of Commons, in the years 1757 and 1758, appointed committees to inquire into the original standards of their weights and measures. These committees, assisted by able mathematicians and artists, examined and compared with each other the several standard measures and weights, and made reports on them in the years 1758 and 1759. The circumstances under which these reports were made entitle them to be considered, as far as they go, as the best written testimony existing of the standard measures and weights of England; and as such, they will be relied on in the progress of this report.'

Jefferson then gave the current units as follows, referring to the pole or perch, which was also known in England as the rod:

'The league of 3 miles,
The mile of 8 furlongs,
The furlong of 40 poles or perches,
The pole or perch of 5^1/$_2$ yards,
The fathom of 2 yards,
The ell of a yard and quarter,
The yard of 3 feet,
The foot of 12 inches, and
The inch of 10 lines.

On this branch of their subject, the committee of 1757–1758, says that the standard measures of length at the receipt of the exchequer, are a yard, supposed to be of the time of Henry VII, and a yard and ell supposed to have been made about the year 1601.'

It is interesting that Jefferson stated that the yard was 'supposed' to date from the time of Henry VII – which means the second half of the 15th century. He appeared to doubt this. Then he said that in 1743 members of the Royal Society had defined English measures from the 'line' (a tenth of an inch) through to the league, by expressing these units as a known part of a 'seconds rod' swung at the latitude of London. Interestingly, there were 10 lines to the inch, 12 inches to the foot and 3 feet to the yard, which meant that the yard contained 360 of the smallest units. This was a rather odd reflection of the Sumerian double-kush which was made up of 360 barley seeds.

Measures of capacity

When Jefferson turned to measures of capacity he defined the volumetric rules for arriving at the specific amount.

'The measures to be made for use, being four sided, with rectangular sides and bottom.

- The pint will be 3 inches square, and $3^3/_4$ inches deep;

- The quart 3 inches square, and $7^1/_2$ inches deep;

- The pottle 3 inches square, and 15 inches deep, or $4^1/_2$, 5, and 6 inches;

- The gallon 6 inches square, and $7^1/_2$ inches deep, or 5, 6, and 9 inches;

- The peck 6, 9, and 10 inches;

- The half bushel 12 inches square, and $7^1/_2$ inches deep; and

- The bushel 12 inches square, and 15 inches deep, or 9, 15, and 16 inches.

Cylindrical measures have the advantage of superior strength, but square ones have the greater advantage of enabling every one who has a rule in his pocket, to verify their contents by measuring them. Moreover, till the circle can be squared, the cylinder cannot be cubed, nor its contents exactly expressed in figures.

Let the measures of capacity, then, for the United States be:

A gallon of 270 cubic inches;

The gallon to contain 2 pottles;

The pottle 2 quarts;

The quart 2 pints;

The pint 4 gills;

Two gallons to make a peck;

Eight gallons a bushel or firkin;

Two strikes, or kilderkins, a coomb or barrel;

Two coombs, or barrels, a quarter or hogshead;

A hogshead and a third one tierce;

Two hogsheads a pipe, butt, or puncheon; and

Two pipes a ton.'

Harmony in the system

The document also records Jefferson's surprise that when he studied the old English measures, that were always described as haphazard and unrelated, he found a curious underlying pattern. He found that the two systems of weights (the avoirdupois and the troy) are the same thing, apart from one being based on the weight of water and the other on the weight of the same volume of wheat grain. Troy weights were still used alongside avoirdupois weights in Jefferson's time and like the avoirdupois weights it is thought that troy weights had originated in the Champagne Fairs, most probably named after 'Troyes', the capital of Champagne. Two differing systems had been very confusing and the English government has already tried unsuccessfully to get rid of one of them:

> 'This seems to have been so combined as to render it indifferent whether a thing were dealt out by weight or measure; for the dry gallon of wheat, and the liquid one of wine, were of the same weight; and the avoirdupois pound of wheat, and the troy pound of wine, were of the same measure.'

The statesman realized something truly remarkable. He was a brilliant man and his document revealed how he had surmised that imperial (or avoirdupois) units were not medieval rough measures as was generally assumed. He was extremely puzzled:

> 'Another remarkable correspondence is that between weights and measures. For 1000 ounces avoirdupois of pure water fill a cubic foot, with mathematical exactness.'

Jefferson could not dismiss this as an amusing coincidence. Everything he had discovered about old measures was revealing a pattern which showed that someone a very, very long time ago had designed this mathematical relationship.

The thoughts of this extraordinary man make for fascinating reading:

'What circumstances of the times, or purposes of barter or commerce, called for this combination of weights and measures, with the subjects to be exchanged or purchased, are not now to be ascertained. But a triple set of exact proportionals representing weights, measures, and the things to be weighed and measured, and a relation so integral between weights and solid measures, must have been the result of design and scientific calculation, and not a mere coincidence of hazard.

It proves that the dry and wet measures, the heavy and light weights, must have been original parts of the system they compose contrary to the opinion of the committee of 1757, 1758, who thought that the avoirdupois weight was not an ancient weight of the kingdom, nor ever even a legal weight, but during a single year of the reign of Henry VIII; and, therefore, concluded, otherwise than will be here proposed, to suppress it altogether. Their opinion was founded chiefly on the silence of the laws as to this weight. But the harmony here developed in the system of weights and measures, of which the avoirdupois makes an essential member, corroborated by a general use, from very high antiquity, of that, or of a nearly similar weight under another name, seem stronger proofs that this is legal weight, than the mere silence of the written laws is to the contrary.'

Jefferson had no doubt that the official explanation for the chaotic origin of the old English weights and measures was completely wrong and based on ignorance of what was obviously once an integrated and precise system. He realized that someone highly advanced from the very distant past must have created a scientific system that had been fragmented, so that its elegance had been lost. We can only speculate on what Jefferson meant by the term 'from high antiquity' but it seems reasonable to assume that he was thinking about the earliest moments of recorded history – or perhaps even before that. He continued to muse over the findings that had surprised him so much.

'Be that as it may, it is in such general use with us, that, on the principle of popular convenience, its higher denominations, at least, must be preserved. It is by the avoirdupois pound and ounce that our citizens have been used to buy and sell... But it will be necessary to refer these weights to a determinate mass of some substance, the specific gravity of which is invariable. Rain water is such a substance, and may be referred to everywhere, and through all time. It has been found by accurate experiments that a cubic foot of rain water weighs 1000 ounces avoirdupois, standard weights of the exchequer. It is true that among these standard weights the committee report small variations; but this experiment must decide in favor of those particular weights, between which, and an integral mass of water, so remarkable a coincidence has been found. To render this standard more exact, the water should be weighed always in the same temperature of air; as heat, by increasing its volume, lessens its specific gravity. The cellar of uniform temperature is best for this also.'

Jefferson's recommendations

Having discovered this inexplicable underlying pattern behind old measures Thomas Jefferson continued with the business of creating new ones. He next defined the dollar:

'Let it be declared, therefore, that the money unit, or dollar of the United States, shall contain 371.262 American grains of pure silver.' [*A grain is a minute subdivision of the pound.*]

The units of decimal length that Jefferson recommended were based on his seconds rod but constructed so that they where close to familiar measurement units:

> 'Let the second rod, then, as before described, be the standard of measure; and let it be divided into five equal parts, each of which shall be called a foot; for, perhaps, it may be better generally to retain the name of the nearest present measure, where there is one tolerably near. It will be about one quarter of an inch shorter than the present foot.
>
> Let the foot be divided into 10 inches;
>
> The inch into 10 lines;
>
> The line into 10 points;
>
> Let 10 feet make a decad;
>
> 10 decads one rood;
>
> 10 roods a furlong;
>
> 10 furlongs a mile.'

While Jefferson's exercise is most impressive, it does show how easy it is for 'improvers' of old systems to lose the core idea. His units of lengths, weight and volume were all based on the Sumerian second of time – but without any understanding of the second's role as a measure of the size and motion of the Earth. The units he proposed would have become total abstractions by moving away from the great, original idea. However, because he used the seconds rod as his basis, he could not avoid being tied into the 'great underlying principle'.

Jefferson's new foot based on one-fifth of the seconds rod was equal to 29.831629 centimetres. He said that there would be 1,000 feet to his furlong and 10,000 to his mile – which is 2,983.1629 metres. This creates the following correspondence:

1,000 Jefferson feet   = 360 Megalithic Yards

What would Thomas Jefferson have thought if he knew that the prehistoric standing stones scattered across the moors of the British Isles had been built with units that were the original mirror image of his 'new' invention? He would have been even more amazed to learn the following:

366 Jefferson furlongs   = 1 Megalithic Degree of arc of the Earth

366^2 Jefferson furlongs   = exact circumference of the Earth

The United States of America did not adopt Jefferson's measures, and that country is now almost alone in using the ancient measurements that so puzzled the man who was to become its third president.

We consider that this work by Jefferson provides us with a winning piece of evidence because the Megalithic 'DNA' is completely present – without the inventor ever realizing it. *The Megalithic Yard is real* and it is the precursor to virtually all major units from history.

It was increasingly obvious to us that the second of time was of great and fundamental importance. It has been universally adopted yet no-one knows what it is, and few people realize where it came from. We decided to return to the land of Sumer to gain a clearer insight into the minds of the people who developed these units of timekeeping.

Conclusions

◎ In the late 18th century Thomas Jefferson set out to create a new system of weights and measures for the new nation of the United States of America. He recorded how the only conceivable starting point for the measure of any dimension was the turning of the Earth – just as we had concluded. Then, just like the Megalithic people and the Sumerians before him he decided that a pendulum was the only way to monitor the spin of the planet.

◎ Because Jefferson adopted a second as the time interval for his pendulum he, like the French, was automatically linking himself with the underlying structure of the Sumerian system. He then made a major improvement in the process by following the discovery of fellow countryman Mr Leslie ('an ingenious artist of Philadelphia'), who identified that a fine, ridged rod used instead of a string on a pendulum would have much more accurate results. Such a rod would not need a weight on the end and it would have to be half as long again as a string pendulum to produce the same swing period.

This led to a rod that was a fraction under 1.5 metres, at 149.158 centimetres – almost exactly three Sumerian kush. Jefferson then divided this rod into five parts to create a new unit he called a 'foot'. He then stated that there would be 1,000 such feet to his proposed furlong.

◎ Unbeknown to the man who was to become third president of his fledgling nation, his foot and furlong taken from the second of time was directly related to the Megalithic and Sumerian systems; 366 Jefferson furlongs are the same as a Megalithic Degree of arc of the Earth and 366^2 Jefferson furlongs describe the exact circumference of the Earth. He had never considered the size of the Earth, so it is now clear that the second of time is, in some way, intrinsically related to the dimensions of our planet.

◎ The next step was for Jefferson to define new weights and capacities which he did by means of cubing his linear units. In the course of conducting this work he studied existing measures and, in doing so, detected that there was some ancient pattern underpinning units which were previously (and still are) thought to be random accidents of history. In finding that a cubic imperial foot held precisely 1,000 ounces he deduced that this was not coincidence but due to some extremely ancient design.

◎ He also identified that the two systems of weights (the avoirdupois and the troy) were not separate systems as generally assumed, but two halves of some single ancient system – one based on the weight of water and the other on the weight of the same volume of wheat grain. Jefferson mused on what far-distant circumstances had led to the creation of such an ancient integrated system, saying that it was the result of 'design and scientific calculation' rather than coincidence.

◎ One of the great men of American history had, like us, found that there was once a highly-developed system of weights and measures that had become fragmented over the course of a very long period of time.

CHAPTER 7

Grains of Ancient Truth

We felt strongly that we would have worked well with Thomas Jefferson. His approach to history was as pragmatic as it was open-minded and he clearly had no reservations about publishing his observations. But his calculations regarding the relative weight and volume relationship between cereal grains and water were distinctly different to our own.

We had found that all grains, whether barley, wheat or rice behave in a very predictable way when poured into a cube-shaped container. Experiments had shown that the shape of the seeds causes them to occupy a volume that is 125 percent that of the same weight of water, which in reverse meant that an equal volume of seeds weighs 20 percent less than water. The 4 x 4 x 4 Megalithic Inch cube proved to hold an imperial pint of water but when the same cube was filled with barley grains it weighed exactly one imperial (or avoirdupois) pound. We also found that the same cube filled with wheat also produced a quantity of wheat that weighed one pound, even though the seeds were a different shape and size than the barley.

Successive experiments demonstrated that the process also worked with rye and with whole rice, although not with polished rice or pearl barley (in which the shape of each seed has been altered by polishing). Our practical experiments were very simple and the results were very clear and yet Jefferson had reported a different relationship between water and wheat. This was a dilemma because we could not see where we could have made an error and it seemed unlikely that a man of Jefferson's abilities was wrong. Could the differences be reconciled?

Avoirdupois and troy weights

Jefferson's report identifies that there were two separate systems of weights in use in the United States at that time, the one called avoirdupois, the other troy. Jefferson explains them as follows:

'In the Avoirdupois series:

The pound is divided into 16 ounces;

The ounce into 16 drachms;

The drachm into 4 quarters.

In the Troy series:

The pound is divided into 12 ounces;

The ounce (according to the subdivision of the apothecaries) into 8 drachms;

The drachm into 3 scruples;

The scruple into 20 grains.

According to the subdivision for gold and silver, the ounce is divided into twenty pennyweights, and the pennyweight into 24 grains.

So that the pound troy contains 5760 grains, of which 7000 are requisite to make the pound avoirdupois; of course the weight of the pound troy is to that of the pound avoirdupois as 5760 to 7000, or as 144 to 175.'

Then, as now, it was normal to assume that the two systems were accidents of history, from different origins with no relationship between them, but Jefferson could see that there was a rather interesting ratio of 144:175. He explains why this caught his attention:

'It is remarkable that this is exactly the proportion of the ancient liquid gallon of Guildhall of 224 cubic inches, to the corn gallon of 272; for 224 is to 272 as 144 to 175.' [*The gallon of Guildhall was an ancient standard gallon kept at the Guildhall in London.*]

Here Jefferson had identified that the relationship between the avoirdupois pound, as used today, and the troy pound exhibit the same relationship as between liquid and grain measures. He was highly surprised to discover this and went on to explain that this links up various measures from the past:

'It is further remarkable still, that this is also the exact proportion between the specific weight of any measure of wheat, and of the same measure of water; for the statute bushel is of 64 pounds of wheat. Now as 144 to 175, so are 64 pounds to 77.7 pounds; but 77.7 pounds is known to be the weight of 2150.4 cubic inches of pure water, which is exactly the content of the Winchester bushel, as declared by the statute…[*Winchester weights and measures were very ancient and though from a different city, had been used in London when the London standards had been lost or became corrupt.*] That statute determined the bushel to be a cylinder of 18$\frac{1}{2}$ inches diameter, and 8 inches depth. Such a cylinder, as nearly as it can be cubed, and expressed in figures, contains 2150.425 cubic inches…We find, then, in a continued proportion 64 to 77.7 as 224 to 172, and as 144 to 175, that is to say, the specific weight of a measure of wheat, to that of the same measure of water, as the cubic contents of the wet gallon, to those of the dry; and as the weight of a pound troy to that of a pound avoirdupois.'

So, Jefferson had identified a relationship between wheat and water that is a ratio of 144:175, which means that he discovered that water is just over 21.5 percent heavier than grain for a known capacity. Yet our practical experiments with cubes of a given volume had revealed a relationship between wheat grain and water of 4:5 – i.e. water is 25 percent heavier than wheat grain.

Using his analysis Jefferson then commented as to how these units must once have been used before the relevance became lost:

'This seems to have been so combined as to render it indifferent whether a thing were dealt out by weight or measure; for the dry gallon of wheat, and the liquid one of wine, were of the same weight; and the avoirdupois pound of wheat, and the troy pound of wine, were of the same measure. Water and the vinous liquors, which enter most into commerce, are so nearly of a weight, that the difference, in moderate quantities, would be neglected by both buyer and seller; some of the wines being a little heavier, and some a little lighter, than water.'

Who was right –Thomas Jefferson or ourselves?

Cubes and cylinders

We rechecked our cube calculations once again and could find no errors. But Jefferson had told us that he used cylinders ('Such a cylinder, as nearly as it can be cubed.') We therefore conducted the experiment with cylinders instead of cubes and found that he was quite correct. The conclusion is that grain behaves very differently in a cube-shaped container than it does in a cylinder of the same volume. Strangely, a cube holds 3.47 percent more grain than a cylinder and we assume this must be due to the way the grains interlock differently where corners are involved.

Understanding the volume of a cylinder requires a knowledge of pi and the use of an arithmetical calculation, which implies a more recent origin than the use of cubes. The Megalithic people did not have a notation system and would have been obliged to use cubes but peoples from the Sumerians onwards could easily have used cylinders. There are therefore two traditions, both of which are derived from the relative weights of wet and dry goods based on grain and water – one using cubes and the other using cylinders. But the importance of grain in all measurement systems is now very clear.

Sumerian mythology has passed into numerous cultures and sacred texts, including the Bible. Over the last decade, Chris has researched these very carefully. In particular, he has made an in-depth study of Enoch, a character who appears in the Old Testament of the Bible and in the 2nd century BC document known as The Book of Enoch.

The Book of Enoch tells us that this great-grandfather of Noah was taught highly-advanced astronomy by a person known as Uriel, apparently at the time that the Megalithic builders were at their peak. In another apocryphal Jewish book, known as The Second Book of Esdras, one section deals with the dead, asking how long they have to wait in their 'secret chambers' before they will be resurrected and can be delivered up from their hidden places. Uriel answers them:

'Even when the number of seeds is filled in you: for He hath weighed the world in the balance. By measure hath He measured the times, and by number hath He measured the times; and He doth not move nor stir them, until the said measure be fulfilled.'

We can be confident that this dates from an extremely archaic period because it is accepted that it was an oral tradition long before it was actually written down. Here Uriel talks of weighing the world and measuring time and quantity.

Barley grains were of great importance to the Sumerians and to all cultures thereafter as a means of measurement – something our newest American associate clearly understood. After some experimentation, we had successfully resolved the potential problem of our 'disagreement' with Thomas Jefferson regarding the relative weight of wheat grains.

Conclusions

◎ Thomas Jefferson had identified a relationship between wheat and water that was a ratio of 144:175 – whereby water is just over 21.5 percent heavier than grain for a known capacity. This was at odds with our practical experiments with cubes which had shown a relationship between wheat grain and water of 4:5, with water being 25 percent heavier than wheat grain. This was reconciled by the fact that we had used cubes and Jefferson had used cylinders of known volumes. Barley and wheat obviously compact quite differently in the two kinds of container. This indicates that cylinders have been used for establishing capacities and weights for a very long time indeed.

◎ The Sumerians/Babylonians used the barley seed as their smallest unit of weight and of linear measure. Ancient documents talk of the world being measured in barley seeds.

CHAPTER 8

The Weight of the World

Alan began to feel somewhat haunted by the words of the angel Uriel in the ancient Book of Enoch:

'...for He hath weighed the world in the balance.'

He began to reflect on the idea of 'weighing the world' and decided to run through some rather unusual calculations. He began by looking up the total mass of the Earth and found that this is now generally quoted as being 5.9763×10^{24} kilograms.[1] Written as a conventional number this would be: 5,976,300,000,000,000,000,000,000 kg.

Alan then converted the number into Sumerian units of weight. We had already established that this unit of weight was arrived at by taking one-tenth of the length of the double-kush or barley cubit and by making a cube with this dimension. The weight is determined by filling such a cube with water. The mass of the water then becomes the Sumerian unit of mass – the double-mana. The double-mana weighed 996.4 grams so there are 5.9979×10^{24} double-manas in the planet's

---

[1] New York Public Library: *Science Desk Reference*. Macmillan, New York, 1995.

mass, which can be seen as 5,997,600,000,000,000,000,000,000 double-mana. This number is as close to 6 followed by 24 zeros as to stand out as being very odd indeed, particularly bearing in mind that we could not be certain as to the 'exact' intended size of the double-kush. Of course, it could be a coincidence but it remains a fact that the weight of the world is only one part out in 2,850 from being precisely:

6,000,000,000,000,000,000,000,000 Sumerian double-manas.

If it were not for the fact that this number conforms so spectacularly to the Sumerian/Babylonian base 60 system of counting we would not have reported it. But it is a tantalizing thought that this ancient unit may have a relationship to the mass of the Earth, either by some brilliant calculation or due to some practical experiment that produced the result by a mechanism unknown to the originators – or to the modern world. Furthermore, we knew that the Sumerians considered that there were 21,600 barley seeds to one double-mana so we can also venture to say that the entire planet is equal to $1,296 \times 10^{26}$ barley seeds – which then gives the following result:

One degree slice of the Earth	=	360×10^{24} barley seeds
One minute slice of the Earth	=	6×10^{24} barley seeds
One second slice of the Earth	=	10^{23} barley seeds

So, a one-second wide section of our planet weighs the same as an incredibly neat 100,000,000,000,000,000,000,000 barley seeds. Simply astonishing!

Again, all of this is entirely consistent with the numbering system used by the Sumerian civilization.

The mass of the Earth

It looked to us as if this was a system of measurement that was designed with the mass of the Earth as its starting point. We therefore decided to try the process from the beginning, as though we were creating new units from some progenitor measurement system:

Step 1: Divide the known mass of the Earth into 6×10^{24} units. This gives us a theoretical unit that equals 996 grams.

Step 2: Establish a size for a cube that holds 996 grams of water. Such a cube would have sides of 9.986648849 centimetres.

Step 3: Take the length of the cube's side to be one-tenth that of a new linear unit. This unit would therefore be 99.86648849 centimetres.

Now we have designed our own new unit of length derived from the exact mass of the Earth and using the Sumerian decimal/sexagesimal principle. How does it compare to reality?

The best estimate of the Sumerian double-kush was taken from studying the rule carved into the statue of King Gudea which gave a length of 99.88 centimetres. The difference between the double-kush and our hypothetical unit of length is therefore 0.1351151 of a millimetre – less than a hair's breadth! This amazing fit may well say more about the skills of the archaeologists who studied Gudea's statue than anything else.

We had to remind ourselves that this could still be a coincidence, however wonderful the fit with Sumerian mathematics. But then we tried another oddball calculation: 'How', we wondered, 'would the imperial pound fit into the mass of the Earth?' – remembering that the pound was produced by a one-tenth Megalithic Yard cube filled with barley seeds.

Starting again with the mass of the Earth at 5.9763 x 10^{24} kilograms we converted into modern (avoirdupois) pounds, which gave a figure of 1.31,754 x 10^{25} pounds. This was another large and apparently meaningless number, so Alan divided it by 366 to find the number of pounds in a one Megalithic degree slice of the Earth. Alan's calculator threw up the answer – 35,998,360,655,737,704,918,033 pounds.

This was a startling result. Alan divided again by 60 to get the result for a 'minute' slice. The numerals this time read: 599,972,677,595, 628,415,300.

Now he completed the sequence by dividing by 6 to find the number of pounds in a Megalithic-second section of the entire planet (which would be 366 Megalithic Yards wide at the equator). The result was: 99,995,446,265,938,069,217.

Suddenly the entirely random numbers from the metric system had blossomed into beautiful near-perfect integers – whole numbers of extraordinary roundness. The weight of the world is defined by the Megalithic system combined with the imperial pound because the following is absolutely true!

> 1 Megalithic-degree section
> of the Earth   = 360×10^{20} pounds
>
> 1 Megalithic-minute section
> of the Earth   = 6×10^{20} pounds
>
> 1 Megalithic-second section
> of the Earth   = 10^{20} pounds

The bottom line is that the modern pound weight is one 100,000,000,000,000,000,000th part of a slice of the Earth one Megalithic second wide at the equator! The accuracy is as good as it gets, since there is a correspondence greater than 99.995 percent –

which boils down to a deviation of one part in 20,000 against science's modern estimates for the mass of the Earth (5.9763×10^{24} kilograms). What is more, when the mass of our planet is viewed in terms of imperial pounds, the result reveals an exact fit with the Megalithic geometry we have already established, just as the result for the Mesopotamian calculation was a classical sexagesimal pattern such as the Sumerians devised.

This could still be a double, outrageous coincidence but the odds against both systems fitting like a near-perfect glove and bearing in mind the Sumerian base 60 method of calculation, made it seem impossible. Somebody in the distant past appears to have known the mass of the Earth to a very accurate number.

The 'Watchers'

Taking stock of what we had found was very challenging. Our concerns about the improbability of the Sumerians having been able to create such a holistic and elegant system were becoming very strong at this point. The relationship of the pound weight and the double-mana (virtually a kilogram) to the mass of the Earth did not seem compatible with the level of sophistication of either the Megalithic people or the Sumerians. Could some other unknown group have developed the principles we see in use and then taught them to these fledgling cultures? Is mankind's leap across the Great Wall of History due to some super-culture that has left no other trace of itself? For the first time we began to theorize about the strange possibility of a group whose existence can only be deduced by the knowledge they left behind. For want of a precise term we began to call them simply 'Civilization One'.

These may sound like foolish thoughts to some, but we have to wonder whether ancient records are true – because they say that is exactly what did happen! Early Sumerian texts, including the famous poem 'The Epic of Gilgamesh', talk repeatedly of very tall, god-like people who came to live among them whom they called 'the Watchers'. Ancient Jewish documents, including versions of the Bible, also make references to these Sumerian Watchers who are again referred to as gods, angels and 'sons of heaven'. The Book of Enoch tells of how these curious people would send teams from unknown points of origin to teach men new skills before mysteriously leaving again. Uriel, the 'angel' who taught Enoch about complex astronomy, is described as one of these Watchers.[2]

The Dead Sea Scrolls also make many references to the Sumerian oral tradition of the Watchers including an episode where Noah's father Lamech becomes concerned that his child is so beautiful that his wife, Bitenosh may have had intercourse with a Watcher.[3] Chapter 6 of The Book of Enoch even names some of the Watchers and gives their specialist subjects:

> 'Semjaza taught enchantments, and root-cuttings, Armarous the resolving of enchantments, Baraquijal astrology, Kokabel the constellations, Ezeqeel the knowledge of the clouds, Araqiel the signs of the earth, Shamsiel the signs of the sun, and Sariel the course of the moon.'

Could it be that once again these ancient documents mean exactly what they say? Did some unknown group act as a catalyst for the world's first known civilization?

Throughout our investigation we have tried not to prejudge what is, and is not, possible for an ancient culture to achieve. We have simply tried to let the data lead us to wherever it takes us. But at this point we were starting to get cold feet. We seemed to be uncovering complexities that surely must have come from a highly-developed society with advanced scientific abilities. With this uncomfortable thought in our minds we decided to try the most obvious next experiment involving the most fundamental property of the universe – the speed of light.

The speed of light

Could the Sumerians possibly have understood how fast light travels? According to current knowledge light travels at 299,792,458 metres per second in a vacuum, which translates to Sumerian units as 600,305,283 kush. However, we cannot be certain that the Sumerians used exactly the second that we do today. It would only have to have drifted by eight ten-thousandths of a second to give a perfect fit to the speed of light. Here again is a Sumerian-style decimal/sexagesimal construction that fits our modern measurements so incredibly closely. The margin of error was almost exactly the same tiny deviation we had found with the mass of the Earth and the Sumerian unit of weight. We remembered that the Sumerians had originally had a double-second and it followed that the same number of double-kushes would apply to the double-second.

Once again, in isolation this result could be a coincidence and normal logic would demand that it *has* to be a coincidence because the Sumerians simply could not know as much as we do. But we soon found good grounds to accept that this result was no mere happenstance.

We decided to look at what is known of the speed of our own planet as it orbits the Sun and found that the near-perfect circle of the Earth's path is 938,900,000,000 metres, which is covered in a year of 365.2596425 days. [4] These numbers look remarkably unimpressive but

2 The Book of Enoch: Chapters 72–82

3 Vermes, G.: The Dead Sea Scrolls: 1QapGen. Penguin, London, 1998.

4 Microsoft® Encarta®, Premium Suite 2003.

the next calculation left us staring at the calculator in disbelief. We were stunned to find that we all travel on our yearly journey at speed of 60,000 kush per second. As a further level of strangeness this speed is a neat one ten-thousandth of the speed of light.

The standard response of mathematicians to numbers that look incredibly neat is to yawn, because they believe that all numbers are equally probable and the actual digits are dependent on the numerical base and the measurement convention employed. They are quite right. But they assume that all measurement units are merely a convention without any underlying physical reality. And that is not the case with either the Megalithic or the Mesopotamian systems.

In this case the second and the kush appear to be very much more than a convenient abstraction because they have all of the characteristics of being fundamental to the realities of the Earth's environment. They have value at a level never conceived of by modern science. We have come to the conclusion that it is more than reasonable to believe that the Sumerians, or more probably their unknown teachers, understood both the mass of the Earth, its orbital speed and even the speed of light, and they designed units that had an integer relationship with them all.

'Civilization One' was moving up our scale of probability from an outside shot to the most reasonable explanation we could imagine.

CONCLUSIONS

◎ We had found that the ancient Mesopotamian unit of measure called the se (barley seed) was a 360th of a double-kush, just as Sumerian records claim.

◎ Taking our lead from ancient texts that refer to weighing the world we were amazed to find that the mass of the Earth is almost perfectly 6×10^{28} Sumerian double-manas. This could be a coincidence but it is a perfect number in the Mesopotamian base 60 system of numbers. This also meant that one second slice of the Earth contains 10^{23} barley seeds.

◎ We next looked at the imperial pound as a potential Megalithic weight and compared it to the mass of the Earth. This produced the astonishingly accurate result where the modern pound weight is one 1,000,000,000,000,000,000,000th part of a slice of the Earth one Megalithic degree wide at the equator.

◎ For both the Sumarian and the Megalithic systems to produce results like this put coincidence out of the window and for the first time we began to theorize about the strange possibility of an unknown progenitor group of super-scientists we called 'Civilization One'.

◎ We then looked at the speed of light through the atmosphere and found that it is almost exactly 600,000,000 kush per second. Next we looked at the speed of the Earth in its motion around the Sun and found that it was incredibly close to 60,000 kush per second. Once again, a perfect Sumerian number. The great mechanism of the solar system must have been measured a very long time ago and ancient units were derived from this super-knowledge from prehistory.

CHAPTER 9

The Missing Link

Our suspicions about a possible progenitor civilization had to be put aside because we did not want to build up unnecessary scenarios that might colour our data-gathering. At this point we had identified two ancient measurement systems that have remarkable properties but which were both instantly available to any user by simply marking out the turning Earth. The fundamental difference between them was that the Megalithic people employed a 366-degree circle and the Sumerians a 360-degree circle. We now needed to understand better the relationship between the two geometric systems.

There were very strong mathematical links between the two systems, especially the fact that the number 360 is the second most important number in the Megalithic principle because there are 360 Megalithic Seconds of arc to the Megalithic Degree. Although we did not yet have grounds to assume a direct connection between the two systems it seemed highly unlikely that two such similar concepts would have developed independently.

The Minoan civilization

We decided we needed to know whether the systems were two independent entities or whether the Sumerians had designed their approach as an improvement on the Megalithic principle. The only avenue open to us seemed to be a closer examination of the Minoan system of measurement used in Crete. There was every reason to believe that the Megalithic 366-degree circle had been adopted and used as the basis of the Minoan foot.

Minoan Crete is widely acknowledged to be Europe's first true civilization. The island, which is located towards the eastern end of the Mediterranean Sea, has given rise to many folk stories of a fabulous culture. Before the beginning of the 20th century, most of these tales were thought to be nothing but myths. It is predominantly down to the efforts of English archaeologist Sir Arthur Evans that the Minoans stepped out of the storybook and became a hard and fast historical reality.

Evans was born in 1851 in Nash Mills, England. He was educated at Harrow and then Brasenose College, Oxford, before settling down to a career as a historian and archaeologist. Evans was fascinated by the heroic accounts of Greek literature and was particularly captivated by constant references to a people of obvious intelligence, political influence and economic power who had supposedly flourished in Crete. Evans visited Crete for the first time in 1894 and was able to obtain and study a number of unknown scripts that had come to light in various places on the island. He was told local folk tales about a wonderful palace that had existed near the north coast of Crete, close to the modern capital of Heraklion.

The German-born Heinrich Schliemann was already famous for his discovery of Troy, at Hissarlik, Turkey in about 1870. His appetite whetted, Schliemann was also on the trail of the ancient Cretan civilization.

Above: The Ring of Brodgar, Scotland. It was Alexander Thom's fascination with the Ring of Brodgar as a young man that led him to a lifelong mission to survey Megalithic structures.

Below: Stonehenge on Salisbury Plain in England is probably the best known of all the Megalithic monuments in the world.

Above: Newgrange in Ireland's Boyne Valley was designed with a 'light box' that gave our ancient ancestors the ability to precisely measure astronomical events.

Below: The first pendulums may have been simply pebbles with holes or clay balls threaded onto twine or sinew.

Above: An exact reproduction of the pottery created by the Grooved Ware people of Great Britain. (circa 3000 BC)

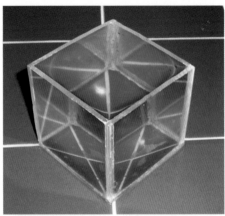

Top: A modern reproduction of a cube with sides of one tenth Megalithic Yard, holding 1 imperial pint of water.

Above: A modern reproduction of a cube with sides of one tenth Megalithic Yard, holding 1 avoirdupois pound of barley.

Left: A simple clay cube, manufactured with sides of one tenth Megalithic Yard.

Top Left: A Sumerian diorite statue of King Gudea who ruled the city state of Lagash (circa 2050–2000BC). Two statues of Gudea, discovered by the French archaeologist Ernest de Sarzec contained examples of a half-kush (barley cubit) measure.

Left: The kush or barley cubit is equal to around 180 barley seeds, even using modern strains of barley.

Below left: The barley inch. In Old English measurements it was said that 3 barley seeds measured 1 inch but the Sumerians laid their barley seeds on their sides for the purpose of linear measurements.

Bottom left: Careful measurement of both the size and weight of barley seeds demonstrates that what the Sumerians claimed about barley seeds was absolutely correct.

Right: The ruins of the Minoan Palace of Knossos in Crete. The Minoans used Megalithic geometry and devised a linear unit known as the Minoan foot that was 1,000th of a second of Earth arc.

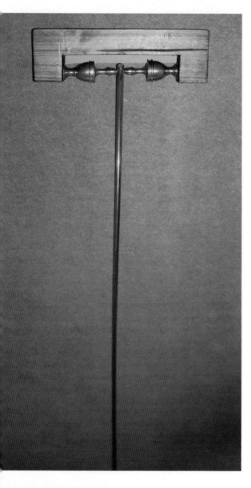

Above: Thomas Jefferson (1743–1826). Jefferson was the author of the American Declaration of Independence and the third President of the United States. He proposed a new system of weights and measures that, unknowingly to him, integrated precisely with the 5,000-year-old Megalithic system.

Left: Thomas Jefferson proposed using a unit of length defined by a rigid pendulum (a rod) which would beat at a one-second interval.

Above: The Phaistos Disc was discovered at the beginning of the 20th century in Phaistos, Crete. Alan Butler's investigations into this previously undeciphered artefact began the search for an alternative geometry based on circles of 366 degrees.

Above: The Megalithic Yard was created from a precise understanding of the dimensions of the Earth. The Megalithic measuring system also defines the mass of the Earth in units identical to the modern pound.

Left: The Moon, the strangest of all the bodies in the solar system, has a circumference that is perfectly described by the Megalithic system of geometry and measurement.

Right: A solar eclipse as seen from Earth. The precise size and position of Earth's Moon allows this most remarkable phenomenon to take place.

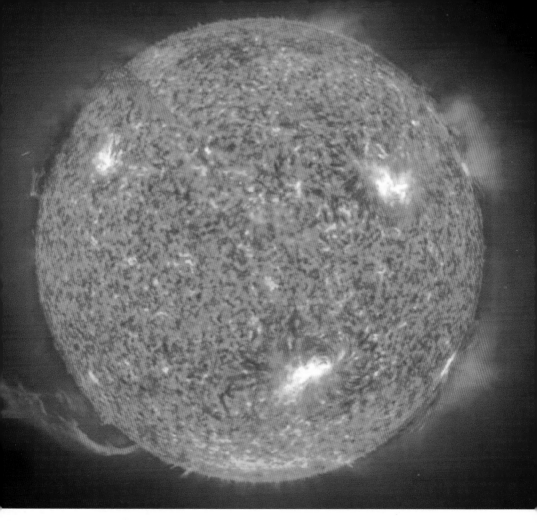

Above: The Sun, standing at the centre of the solar system, is 400 times larger than the Moon and 400 times further from the Earth. It is also perfectly described by Megalithic geometry.

Above: The Planet Venus was held as sacred to many ancient cultures. It was used by both the Megalithic peoples of Britain and France and by the Sumerians to establish the length of their respective units of linear length, using visual observations and pendulums.

The Relationship Between Music and Visible Light

Probable extent of visible light

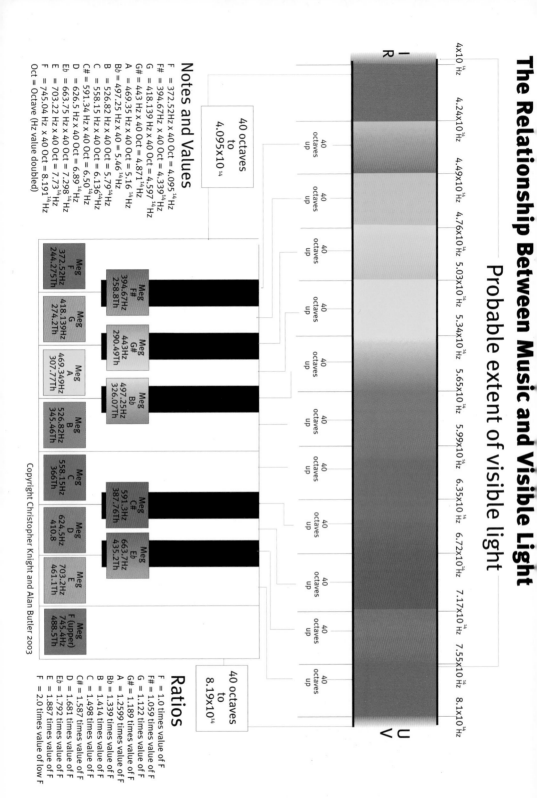

Notes and Values

F = 372.52Hz x 40 Oct = 4.095 $\times 10^{14}$ Hz
F# = 394.67Hz x 40 Oct = 4.339 $\times 10^{14}$ Hz
G = 418.139 Hz x 40 Oct = 4.597 $\times 10^{14}$ Hz
G# = 443 Hz x 40 Oct = 4.871 $\times 10^{14}$ Hz
A = 469.35 Hz x 40 Oct = 5.16 $\times 10^{14}$ Hz
Bb = 497.25 Hz x 40 = 5.46 $\times 10^{14}$ Hz
B = 526.82 Hz x 40 Oct = 5.79 $\times 10^{14}$ Hz
C = 558.15 Hz x 40 Oct = 6.136 $\times 10^{14}$ Hz
C# = 591.34 Hz x 40 Oct = 6.50 $\times 10^{14}$ Hz
D = 626.5 Hz x 40 Oct = 6.89 $\times 10^{14}$ Hz
Eb = 663.75 Hz x 40 Oct = 7.298 $\times 10^{14}$ Hz
E = 703.22 Hz x 40 Oct = 7.73 $\times 10^{14}$ Hz
F = 745.04 Hz x 40 Oct = 8.191 $\times 10^{14}$ Hz
Oct = Octave (Hz value doubled)

Ratios

F = 1.0 times value of F
F# = 1.059 times value of F
G = 1.122 times value of F
G# = 1.189 times value of F
A = 1.2599 times value of F
Bb = 1.339 times value of F
B = 1.414 times value of F
C = 1.498 times value of F
C# = 1.587 times value of F
D = 1.681 times value of F
Eb = 1.792 times value of F
E = 1.887 times value of F
F = 2.0 times value of low F

40 octaves to 4.095x10^{14}

40 octaves to 8.19x10^{14}

40 octaves up (×11)

4x10^{14} Hz	
4.24x10^{14} Hz	
4.49x10^{14} Hz	
4.76x10^{14} Hz	
5.03x10^{14} Hz	
5.34x10^{14} Hz	
5.65x10^{14} Hz	
5.99x10^{14} Hz	
6.35x10^{14} Hz	
6.72x10^{14} Hz	
7.17x10^{14} Hz	
7.55x10^{14} Hz	
8.1x10^{14} Hz	

Meg F 372.52Hz 244.275Th
Meg F# 394.67Hz 258.8Th
Meg G 418.139Hz 274.2Th
Meg G# 443Hz 290.49Th
Meg A 469.349Hz 307.77Th
Meg Bb 497.25Hz 326.07Th
Meg B 526.82Hz 345.46Th
Meg C 558.15Hz 366Th
Meg C# 591.3Hz 387.76Th
Meg D 624.5Hz 410.8
Meg Eb 663.7Hz 435.2Th
Meg E 703.2Hz 461.1Th
Meg F (upper) 745.4Hz 488.5Th

I R

U V

The spectrum from music to light. This diagram demonstrates how the frequency of musical notes, when doubled 40 times, provide a frequency that falls within the spectrum of visible light.

He attempted to purchase a large area of ground on an important hill not far from Heraklion, but was unable to reach an agreement with the owners. Perhaps it is fortunate for archaeology that this was the case, because the more patient and less destructive Arthur Evans eventually took possession of the site in question and uncovered the Palace of Knossos. The work Evans undertook at Knossos for the remainder of his life was long and hard but slowly and surely he was able to resurrect the lost culture, throwing more light on a generally dim European prehistory. Subsequent discoveries elsewhere in Crete have produced an even greater understanding of the Minoan civilization – a name that Evans had given to this people on account of its fabled king Minos.

We now know that the Minoan culture was thriving during the period that corresponds to the later Neolithic Period in the British Isles and that the civilization reached its peak shortly after 2000 BC. The archaeological record reflects a strong, vibrant, freedom-loving and fiercely independent people that developed strong international trade and whose sailors were possibly the most accomplished seafarers of their day. The Minoans were also tremendously creative. They made fine pottery and adorned the walls of their palaces with colourful frescoes. They exported honey, pottery, wine and craftwork in great quantities, establishing settlements in many places along the north coast of the Mediterranean and into the Aegean. Imports included copper, tin and other metals not available on Crete itself.

Life on the island was good, with a populace that seems to have supported a religious and civil elite that held its power through common consensus rather than through military strength. Although the Minoan navy swept the seas around its shores free of pirates, Crete never seems to have had a standing army and none of the excavated buildings from the period possessed any form of fortification. Most of the Minoans appear to have been free and independent, merely paying a tribute in goods to the several palaces where vast magazines (store houses) have been excavated, indicating storage of all the necessities of life on a grand scale.

In a religious sense, it is clear that the people of Crete had adopted the nature-based beliefs that seem to have been commonplace in Europe and parts of Asia since the Neolithic dawn. The predominant deity appears to have been an 'Earth goddess' whose place in religion was paramount, though she had a consort who was first her son and then her husband. The god was born, grew and died in a cyclic way, whereas the goddess was perpetual. Perhaps as a response to this form of religion, Minoan women seemed to have had some power in their society and it has even been suggested that the civil administration was geared in their direction rather than in that of men. It is now recognized that Minoan Crete was the cradle of the religious thinking that would eventually predominate on the Greek mainland, though by that time it had changed its nature to a much more male-dominated belief pattern.

How far Minoan civilization might have come and the part it could have played in building the modern world is somewhat academic, because tragedy struck this culture. About 60 miles to the north of Crete was an important Minoan settlement on the small, volcanic island of Santorini, also known as Thera. In approximately 1450 BC the island exploded with such ferocity that much of it simply ceased to exist. Undoubtedly the explosion led to catastrophic tidal waves and also to a fall of ash that would have rendered the fields of at least northern Crete barren for as much as a decade.[1]

It was at about this time that Crete fell under the influence and

[1] Phillips, G.: *Act of God*. Sidgwick and Jackson, London, 1998.

ultimately the rule of a very different culture which had been developing on the Greek mainland. This was a civilization that would come to be called Mycenae. The Mycenaeans were far more warlike than the Minoans and, over a prolonged period, they had captured a number of cities around their own base at Mycenae. Eventually their dominance of Crete changed the gentle and more creative Minoan way of life into something far more aggressive. Influence worked both ways, however. Minoan sensibility is readily obvious in Mycenaean culture, art, building techniques and religion. Since the Mycenaeans offered much to what would become the people we know as the Ancient Greeks, it is now taken for granted that Minoan ideas lasted long after the civilization itself had fallen into decay.

During the 1960s, Canadian archaeologist J. Walter Graham conducted a series of experiments at the ruins of the Minoan palaces of Crete. These were at Knossos, Phaistos and Malia, where Graham was trying to establish whether or not the Minoans had used a basic unit of linear measurement in their buildings. As we have already discussed in Chapter 2, Graham was able to show that the Minoan builders had used a standard unit that was 30.36 centimetres – a unit he dubbed the 'Minoan foot'.

The Phaistos Disc

Alan had become particularly interested in the Minoans due to a small clay disc found in the ruins of one of the Minoan palaces, which was dated as circa 2000 BC. This artefact, known as the Phaistos Disc, was carefully analysed by Alan and it was the results of this study that had led to his first observation regarding the use of a 366-day year and 366-degree circle. The disc is a rather sophisticated ready-reckoner with a primary function that seems to have been to synchronize the ritual year of 366 days with the true solar year of 365.25 days. There are drawings of the Phaistos Disc and a longer explanation of Alan's findings in Appendix 5.

Alan had already seen a potential connection between the mathematical principles evident in the Phaistos Disc and those associated with the Megalithic Yard before he came across Graham's work on the Minoan foot. It was a startling revelation when we realized that 366 Megalithic Yards was the same thing as 1,000 Minoan Feet.

Megalithic, Minoan and Olympic measurements

Since 366 Megalithic Yards also represents 1 Megalithic Second of arc of the Earth's polar circumference, it seemed safe to suggest that the Minoans had used Megalithic geometry when creating this unit. That the culture had contact with their Megalithic contemporaries to the west, is not a contentious point as there are many artefacts that point to a trading relationship between the two lands. A number of artefacts have been found in the south of England, some on Salisbury Plain close to Stonehenge, which include cups, rings and other examples of jewellery which were originally identified as being Mycenaean in origin. Later investigations showed that the Mycenaean culture had not existed in the period to which these artefacts were dated. Since much if not all Mycenaean art is Minoan in origin, it is hard to avoid the conclusion that these artefacts were made in Crete during Minoan times.

The Minoans would have had very good reason to visit the shores of Britain, most particularly the tin mines of Cornwall. It was one of the very few sources of tin available to them, and they needed significant quantities of the metal in order to create bronze. But even without the evidence of contact between Britain and Crete, the fit between 366 Megalithic Yards and 1,000 Minoan feet is highly unlikely to be a coincidence.

The culture we now simply call 'the Ancient Greeks' began to form circa 700 BC, following what is often called 'the Greek Dark Age' that had occurred after the destruction of the Mycenaean Empire. Both the Minoan and the Mycenaean civilizations were large components of the foundation blocks for the religious and general cultural heritage of the Ancient Greeks, which in turn has always been seen as perhaps the greatest influence on our own Western culture of today. By the time the Ancient Greek civilization reached maturity its scholars had also been influenced by both Babylonian and Egyptian mathematical thinking. As a result, their experiments into mathematics and geometry were based on the same 360-degree geometrical models favoured by both Babylon and Egypt. It might therefore be expected that all traces of the Megalithic-influenced Minoan system would have vanished from Greece completely. However, a close look at Greek units of weights and measures strongly suggests that this was not the case.

We discovered that there were several forms of foot and cubit in use during the period of the Ancient Greeks. However, one example stands out above the rest, not least because it was the basic unit used in architectural measurement; even today its true nature cannot be doubted. This unit was known as the 'Olympian' or 'Geographical' foot. By general consent, the Olympian foot measured what might at first seem like a meaningless 30.861 centimetres. We immediately noticed something special about the relationship between the Minoan foot and the later Greek foot. To an accuracy of an extremely close 99.99 percent, a distance of 366 Minoan feet is the same as 360 Greek feet! This was incredible, and we felt certain that it was not a coincidence. The two units did not need to have any integer relationship at all – yet they relate to each other in a Megalithic to Sumerian manner:

Minoan foot of 30.36
centimetres   x 366 = 111.1176 metres

Olympian foot of 30.861

centimetres   x 360 = 111.0996 metres

Over a distance of more than 111 metres the difference between the 366/360 fit is just 18 millimetres. Was this the meeting point of the changeover from the old 366 system to a new 360 approach?

Many other researchers have already put forward the idea that the Greek foot was a geodetic unit, that is, related directly to the size of the Earth. Such suggestions are not usually even discussed in the corridors of academia because the existing convention asserts, quite unreasonably, that absolute knowledge of the Earth's dimensions did not come about until more recent times. Such is the power of dogma: it blinds the eyes of even those who are supposedly trained to have the clearest vision. Our approach is not to be bound by academic fashion or current convention, and so we looked with an open mind.

It takes only seconds with a calculator to grasp the fact that there are close to 360,000 Greek feet to 1 degree of the polar circumference of the Earth when using the 360-degree circle.

> **The polar circumference of the Earth is around 40,008 kilometres, which is 40,008,000 metres. A degree is one 360th of this, which is 111,133.33 metres. The Greek foot is 30.861 centimetres in length and this divides into 111,133.33 metres 360,109 times.**

The 360 degrees of the Earth's circumference give us a figure of 129,600,000 Greek feet. Since we have done nothing to massage either the size of the Olympian foot or the dimensions of the Earth, the suggestion that this could be a coincidence has to be rejected by any objective person.

The pattern can be fully appreciated when it is observed how tightly the Greek foot would fit both Earth geometry and time measurement.

1 Greek foot = 30.861 centimetres

100 Greek feet	= 30.8 metres	= 1 second of arc polar circumference
6,000 Greek feet	= 1.85222 kilometres	= 1 minute of arc polar circumference
360,000 Greek feet	= 111.1333 kilometres	= 1 degree of arc polar circumference
129,600,000 Greek feet	= 40,007.988 kilometres	= The polar circumference of Earth

In terms of time, the Greek foot is also more than useful. As the Earth spins on its axis a fixed distance passes at the equator for a known period of time:

1 modern second of time	=	1,500 Greek feet
1 modern minute of time	=	90,000 Greek feet
1 modern hour of time	=	5,400,000 Greek feet
1 day	=	129,600,000 Greek feet

Taking these observations in conjunction with the Sumerian and the Megalithic systems, this confirms our previous conclusion that the dimensions of our planet have been known for thousands of years longer than previously thought. The Greek foot divides into the polar circumference of the Earth in a perfectly rational set of integer numbers.

We know from our own extensive research that the geodetic nature of the Greek Olympian foot has been appreciated for a very long time. The fit is so accurate that it cannot be doubted that those designing this unit of linear measurement not only knew what it could do, but had deliberately *manufactured* it to do that job.

Just as surely as 366 Megalithic Yards are the same as 1,000 Minoan feet, so 366 Minoan feet are equal to 360 Greek feet. Now we really could see the transition between the two systems. But another major issue suddenly became obvious:

The Sumerian numerical system tells us that the following is true:

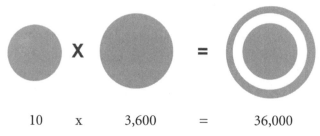

| 10 | x | 3,600 | = | 36,000 |

Sumerian script.

Then the following applies to identify the tenth stage of the numerical system:

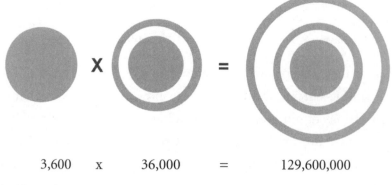

| 3,600 | x | 36,000 | = | 129,600,000 |

Sumerian script.

(These symbols were those actually used by Sumerian scribes. We know full well what they were intended to represent in terms of numbers because of the mathematical problems played out on many clay tablets found in the region. Only the last symbol is of our own invention and is a natural consequence of what goes before.)

The result here is the very important tenth place in the Mesopotamian decimal/sexagesimal counting system, with a value of 129,600,000, which confirms that this was an Earth geometry-based approach. This is the case because, as we have seen above, 129,600,000 is exactly the number of Greek feet in the polar circumference of the Earth. It is probably coincidence but the hieroglyph for this huge number even looks like a globe viewed from above with a pole in the centre, the equator at the edge and the 45-degree latitude in the middle. While the symbol may be coincidence, nobody could seriously dismiss this carefully-crafted system as a being a chance occurrence.

Musing over these findings we found the story of the Greek mathematician Eratosthenes particularly interesting as he is supposed to have been the first person to make a reasonable estimate of the Earth's circumference. Eratosthenes lived in Greek Alexandria about 250 BC, and the story goes that he learned that the Sun, on the day of the summer solstice, shone absolutely vertically down a well in a town called Syene, south of Alexandria. Eratosthenes knew that the Sun never rose high enough to shine straight down a well in Alexandria on the same day, and he worked out that it failed to do so by an angle of seven degrees. From these facts, Eratosthenes was able to deduce that the Earth must be a sphere and he then calculated the size of the terrestrial globe. Considering the potential problems involved, his estimation was surprisingly accurate because he suggested that the Earth was 130,650,335 Olympian feet.

Poor Eratosthenes clearly did not realize that the Olympian foot only existed because someone, maybe thousands of years before him, had measured the size of the Earth and divided it into precisely 129,600,000 parts. He had then innocently and painstakingly reverse-engineered it with his own experiment. It is clear that the Greek culture had already lost contact with the prehistoric origins of the knowledge it possessed, and today history textbooks erroneously describe Eratosthenes as being the first man to measure the globe.

The only major truly ancient civilization we had not yet looked at in detail was that of the Egyptians. We knew the Egyptian cubit was somewhat different to the Mesopotamian kush, so we did not really expect to find significant correspondences with our existing research. How wrong we were.

CONCLUSIONS

◎ Having already established that 1,000 Minoan feet are the same as 366 Megalithic Yards, we found that the much later Olympian foot created by the Greeks (30.861 centimetres) is also related. To an accuracy of an incredible 99.99 percent, a distance of 366 Minoan feet is the same as 360 Greek feet.

◎ This means that there are 100 Greek feet in a second of arc of the Earth's polar circumference and 360,000 in a single degree.

Chapter 10

Widening the Search

The standard view of history is based on the assumption that the further back in time one looks, the greater will be the disorganization. We have found that the opposite is the case – the deeper we peer into the past the greater the harmony. Against a lifetime of conventional training this sounds counterintuitive. It would take a brave academic to challenge the standard paradigm of history and it has been largely left to interested amateurs such as Graham Hancock or Robert Temple (writers and broadcasters) to champion alternative worldviews. Hancock and Temple and others like them are working at the fringes of academic acceptability by looking for new ways to interpret how humanity might have arrived at its present position. Inevitably these people make mistakes, sometimes sizable ones, which give their opponents a stick with which to beat them. Whether Graham Hancock is correct in his assertion that archaeological records indicate the existence of a lost, ancient, global civilization we cannot say, but we are aware that our own, unrelated research is now pointing very powerfully in that direction.

It is now certain that people in the distant past were a great deal cleverer than anyone has so far asumed. However, the process of unravelling the idea that the inhabitants of the British Isles were ignorant and unsophisticated has taken decades, and the battle still lumbers on. More than 40 years ago radio astronomer Professor Gerald Hawkins (late Professor of Physics and Astronomy at Boston University, Massachusetts) used a computer to show that the stones and other archaeological features at Stonehenge formed a pattern of alignments with 12 major lunar and solar events, suggesting that it was used as a Neolithic observatory and astronomical calendar. He identified 165 key points in the complex and found that many were strongly correlated with the rising and setting positions of the Sun and Moon over an 18.03-year cycle. He argued that Stonehenge had once allowed the users to predict eclipses of the Moon as well as the positions of the Sun and Moon at the summer and winter solstices.

Hawkins published his findings in an article, 'Stonehenge Decoded', in the journal *Nature* in 1963 and in a book of the same title two years later. But mainstream archaeologists could not accept the findings because their previous evidence had indicated that the level of sophistication suggested by Hawkins's theory was too advanced for a site of this date. Instead of considering changing their worldview to accommodate new evidence, the natural reaction of the experts was to protect their old ideas by ignoring Hawkins's material or immediately seeking reasons to fault it.

Archaeologists have an absolutely vital role in the academic world and we certainly do not wish to be disrespectful regarding the excellent work they put into understanding past cultures – but is it coincidence that some of the really big breakthroughs have come from people outside the discipline? This seems particularly true when one considers that Hawkins was a radio astronomer and Alexander Thom an engineer.

The holistic study of language

Standard archaeology is highly compartmentalized and connections between cultures divided by time or geography are not approved of without written contemporary evidence or crossover physical artefacts. The only holistic study of which we are aware is that relating to the development of language, which maps out a tree of connections for world languages as they appear now. Today, the people of the world speak more than 6,000 distinct languages, which are grouped into 11 main language families. The Indo-European family represents about 1.6 billion people and includes most of the languages of Europe and northern India, Australia, the United States and parts of South America.

In the 18th century the German philosopher Gottfried Wilhelm Leibniz suggested that all ancient and modern languages diverged from a single protolanguage. This idea, called 'monogenesis', sounds very odd but it is taken very seriously by many leading scholars. Anthropologist and writer Richard Rudgely has said the consequences of acknowledging a root language are mind-boggling. Such a language must be more that 10,000 years old and probably nearer to 15,000 years old. It is amazing that correspondences in language exist as far afield as the deserts of southern Africa, the Amazon rainforest, the Arctic and Europe. Linguist and writer Merrit Ruhlen has called the ancient original language, 'Proto-Global'.[1]

Even academics as revered as Lord Colin Renfrew, Disney Professor of Archaeology at the University of Cambridge, have concluded that every group of humans in the world once spoke the same language – and that the date of this convergence was as recent as 15,000 years ago. These experts follow the patterns of words that are shared by peoples who have no known connection, yet they stop short of asking how such

[1] Ruhlen, M.: 'Linguistic Evidence for Human Prehistory'. *Cambridge Archaeological Journal*, 5/2, 1995.

a thing can be true. Surely, if everyone spoke the same language there must have been a high level of regular contact between peoples around the world, at a time when, in the modern comprehension of prehistory, this would have been impossible?

We have taken a similar approach to that used for tracing the origin of language, but using measurements, astronomical methodologies and geometry instead of words, and these indicate a convergence something over 5,000 years ago.

We had built on Thom's invaluable work to detect strong links in the astronomy-based measurement systems of the Megalithic people of the region centred on the British Isles with the Minoans on Crete, and the Sumerians of present-day Iraq and Kuwait. We now wondered whether the same principles that we had come to call the 'Great Underlying Principle' had been used elsewhere around the world.

The 'Great Underlying Principle' around the world

We turned first to India, where there was a unit of measurement known as the 'gaz', the origins of which are no longer known. It was regularly used in the planning and building of sacred structures, such as temples as far back in time as the Indus Valley Civilization which is usually dated as 2800–1750 BC. Also known as the Harappa culture, it covered a triangular area of some half a million square miles centred on the Indus River that runs from the Himalayas to the Arabian Sea. The time frame of this culture means that it was at its height at about the same time as the Ancient Egyptians and the Sumerians, but a little later than the Megalithic people. It also had a substantial overlap with the Minoan culture.

The gaz was still in use at the time British rule was imposed on India in 1765. To save the British any 'confusion' the gaz was later stan-dardized to match the British yard, but early records suggest that it had originally measured something closer to 33 inches – which is 83.82 centimetres.[2] This approximate length would bring it extremely close to the Megalithic Yard, which is 82.96656 centimetres. More recent excavations have brought to light a number of measures, one of which is the 'Indus inch'. This was 3.35 centimetres, and there were 25 Indus inches to the gaz – suggesting a length of 83.75 centimetres, which is even closer to the definition of the Megalithic Yard. This was interesting, but this near fit could easily be a coincidence and we were not aware of any further evidence to support a link, so it may or may not be connected to the Megalithic system. However, just a few weeks later an article appeared in the magazine *Scientific American* which rekindled our interest in the Harappan culture. It stated that excavations at one of the oldest sites had shown how an economic culture had existed during the Kot Dijian Period (2800–2600 BC). A particularly interesting artefact was a tiny limestone cube that scientists identified as a weight, possibly used for tax or tribute purposes.[3] It weighed 1.13 grams, which directly related it to a series of standard weights used in later Indus valley cities. The interesting point to us was that this weight is one 400th of an imperial pound to a high degree of mathematical exactitude. No-one else would have considered trying to test for a match with modern units of weight because there is no known reason to even suspect that there could be a relationship. However, our research had taught us that the further back one looks the stronger the likelihood of a connection to the Great Underlying Principle.

We looked up the official website associated with the archaeology of the Harappan sites. It showed a picture of such stone cubes arranged in size order and the caption read:

[2] Mackie, E.: *The Megalithic Builders*. Phaidon Press, London, 1977.
[3] Kenoyer, J.M.: 'Uncovering the keys to the lost Indus Cities.' *Scientific American.* Vol. 289, No.1, July 2003.

'... the most common weight is approximately 13.7 grams, which is in the 16th ratio. In the large weights the system becomes a decimal increase where the largest weight is 100 times the weight of the 16th ratio...' [4]

It follows that this 'largest weight' referred to is 1.37 kilograms – which just happens to be three imperial pounds to a great level of accuracy.

We had long since identified that the pound weight can be derived from a one-tenth Megalithic Yard cube and here we see a system that has small weights of one four-hundredth of a pound and large ones which are 1200 times that amount, at three pounds. Coincidence? Possibly – but it seems very unlikely when the old unit of length known as the gaz is brought back into the picture. There is no evidence that we are aware of that gives a precise measure for the gaz but we know it was very close to the Megalithic Yard, which was still in use in Britain when the earliest Indus Valley cities were established. Could international communications have been so advanced as to allow a southern Asian culture to take its measurement system from the Megalithic builders of the western fringes of Europe? Or is it more likely that all the ancient cultures we have looked at had the same teachers? Could an otherwise unknown group of super-scientists, that we have dubbed 'Civilization One' have trained indigenous peoples around the world to accelerate global civilization. It is still very speculative but it is a very convincing solution to a problem that sounds odd to conventionalist ears, even though it is not in the least improbable, let alone impossible. We make no apology for sharing such a radical, even heretical, thought.

Vocalizing these ideas would be highly dangerous for any academic who values their career and peer-group esteem. In academia, only the world of quantum physics has learned that reality is far, far stranger than any science fiction writer could ever imagine.

Continuing our investigation of measurement used by other ancient cultures we next turned away from India and back to Europe. There was once a Castilian Spanish unit of measurement known as the 'vara', which also became popular in Spanish Central America. The vara is generally considered to be equal to 83.5905 centimetres,[5] making it about 0.75 percent larger than the Megalithic Yard.

There are Megalithic structures in Castile but Alexander Thom did not survey them, so we do not know whether the Megalithic Yard was employed there. Old Castile was originally a province of the kingdom of Leon with Burgos as its capital. Today it is central and northern Spain, traditionally divided into Old Castile and New Castile, and now split into Castile-La Mancha and Castile-Leon. It does seem possible that this region could have retained a unit from prehistory but the Spanish vara cannot be confidently considered more than a coincidence without further corroboration, but the strong possibility of a connection remains.

We looked next to the Far East and found that the oldest Japanese measure was known as the 'shaku', which is believed to have been imported from China more than 1,000 years ago. At 30.30 centimetres this unit is almost indistinguishable from a Minoan foot, which is just 0.6 millimetres larger. It follows therefore that 366 Megalithic Yards are almost the same as 1,000 Japanese shaku, with a fit accuracy of 99.8 percent. Connection or coincidence? It could be either, so we decided not to develop this area of investigation unless something new occurred to strengthen the possibility of a connection. The only relatonships with the Megalithic builders of the British Isles and other cultures that could be described as conclusive are with the Minoans, the Sumerians and now the Harappan culture.

[4] http://www.harappa.com/indus/21.html
[5] http://unicon.netian.com/unitsys_e.html#france1

The next civilization we turned to is the most famous of them all – Ancient Egypt. The Ancient Egyptians have long fired the imagination because they left such stunning artefacts behind them – both in terms of scale and beauty. They began their development just on our side of the Great Wall of History and they appeared to blossom from nowhere. There are many pyramids in Egypt but the three splendid ones on the Giza Plateau are by far the most famous, along with the mysterious Sphinx, which sits nearby on the sands of the desert. The largest of the three pyramids is associated with King Khufu and has an estimated volume of some 2.6 million cubic metres. It is believed that 2.5 million blocks of stone, each weighing an average of 2.5 tonnes, were used to build it. Each side of this pyramid is approximately 230 metres long and its height is about 146 metres.

Unquestionably, these 4,300-year-old structures represent an almost superhuman feat of engineering and this obvious skill has caused many people to wonder if such buildings were more than grand burial mounds.

It is universally agreed that Egyptians were good practical astronomers. It has been suggested that some of the mysterious 'shafts' deliberately built into the sides of the Khufu pyramid were specifically angled to cosmological events. If this were the case, it undoubtedly had a religious meaning, because the Egyptians were obsessed with death and the afterlife.

Ancient and modern mathematics

It might be thought that people who could build on such a colossal scale would also be excellent mathematicians and this is true, though only up to a point. Most experts agree that Egyptian expertise with mathematics dealt mainly with the practical aspects of life and did not veer much, or often, into the area of theory (which would become so important to the Ancient Greeks). The Egyptians had a form of geometry, knew how to make right angles and appear to have followed broadly similar principles to their contemporaries, the Sumerians, though without some of the flair exhibited by the mathematicians of Mesopotamia.

It is worth repeating here the fundamental difference between modern mathematics and the mathematics of the ancients. The variety used in the British Isles, Mesopotamia, India and Egypt was what is now known as 'algorithmic mathematics' and that used today (invented by the Greeks) is called 'dialectic mathematics'. The following definitions are provided by Emeritus Professors Philip J. Davis, Brown University, and Reuben Hersh, University of New Mexico.

Algorithmic mathematics as used by the ancient civilizations represents a tool for solving real-world problems. It is concerned not only with the existence of a mathematical object but also with the credentials of its existence. This approach allows mathematics to vary according to the urgency of the problem in hand.

Dialectic mathematics is a rigorously logical science where statements are either true or false and where objects with specified properties either do or do not exist. It is an intellectual game played to rules about which there is widespread consensus. Throughout the 20th century mathematics became increasingly dialectic and many amateur mathematicians have mistakenly assumed it is the best, or even the only form the subject can take.

NASA could never have put a man on the moon if the trajectories had not been computed with dialectic rigour combined with algorithmic pragmatism. In short, dialectic mathematics invites contemplation while algorithmic mathematics invites action and delivers results. We believe that it is fair to say that both approaches have their value and most great achievements required the use of both, though there is also some tension between them. Leading mathematicians Professors Davis and Hersh believe that there is sometimes a conflict in the minds of users:

> 'There is a distinct paradigm shift that distinguishes the algorithmic from the dialectic, and people who have worked in one mode may very well feel that solutions within the second mode are not "fair" or not "allowed". They experience paradigm shock.' [6]

The Ancient Egyptians created the pyramids using an algorithmic approach and it is also true to say that they were fantastic at logistics. They had to be, because gathering perhaps tens of thousands of people together in one place, for example to build a huge pyramid, involved planning on a grand scale. Not only had the craftsmen and work gangs to be organized, but also their raw materials had to be sourced and prepared, and a massive support team would have been needed to feed and water such huge numbers.

What the Egyptians seem to have been less good at was building a calendar that could be said to show a high degree of accuracy to the actual year. The reason for this was no lack of intelligence on the part of the Egyptian astronomer-priests, but rather that it was tied to necessity. It rarely rains in Egypt and the region is not particularly subjected to seasons in the accepted sense of the word. Egypt owed its prosperity to the annual flooding of the Nile, the great river that was the lifeblood of all the towns and cities comprising the civilization.

The River Nile rises many hundreds of kilometres beyond the boundaries of Egypt itself, in areas that do experience significant changes in rainfall. The Egyptians themselves were almost certainly unaware of this fact but they had noticed that the flooding of the Nile

6 Davis, P.J. and Hersh, R.: *The Mathematical Experience*. Penguin Books, London, 1990.

took place each year just after the helical rising (first visible, brief appearance on the eastern horizon before sunrise) of the star Sirius. The Nile flood brought with it extremely fertile silt, which ran across the fields alongside the river. When the flood had receded, crops were planted in the silt and were simply harvested when they had reached maturity. All crops would be harvested well ahead of the next flooding of the Nile, eventually creating a society that was really not at all concerned about tremendous accuracy in terms of the length of the year.

The best the Egyptians ever achieved in terms of a calendar, at least until the time of Alexander the Great, was to celebrate a 360-day year, with 5 extra days each year added as holidays. The true solar year is 365.2564 days in length, so every year the Egyptian calendar was out by over a quarter of a day. Nobody cared much, just as long as those dedicated to watching for the event saw the helical rising of Sirius and alerted everyone to the fact.

It is certain that Egyptian scholars were good at dealing with areas and volumes, in fact any aspect of mathematics that had a sound, practical reason, though the methods used developed early and did not move forward for well over 2,000 years. By inference, the Egyptians probably knew about a 360-degree circle, though they never seem to have understood its significance in the way the Sumerians did because they opted very early in their history for a 24-hour day, which essentially divorces the measurement of time and Earth geometry. There is no evidence we are aware of to suggest that the Egyptians knew of, or cared about, the Sumerian second or minute of time.

The 'DNA' of the Great Underlying Principle

What we wanted to know was whether any aspect of Egyptian measures carried any of the 'DNA' of the Great Underlying Principle we had identified among the Megalithic folk and the Sumerians. Looking at the available information it seemed as though neither Megalithic geometry nor its linear measurements were known to the Ancient Egyptians.

The basic unit of linear measurement in use for nearly the whole of Egyptian history was the 'royal cubit'. Opinions vary very slightly on the length of this unit, some putting it at 52.372 centimetres and others at 52.35 centimetres, while Professor Livio Stecchini considered it to be about 52.4 centimetres. He concluded that the length of the sides of Khufu's pyramid (also known as the Pyramid of Cheops) was intended to be 230,560 millimetres and after exhaustive research he went on to state:

> 'It is agreed amongst serious scholars that the side was calculated as 440 Egyptian royal cubits. Borchardt drew the conclusion that the cubit had a length of 523.55 mm, but in my opinion, one must take into account the difficulty of proceeding in a perfectly straight line without telescopic instruments. Cole, as an experienced surveyor, calls attention to this factor. Since other dimensions, such as those of the King's Chamber, indicate the use of a cubit very close to 524 mm, one can assume that the theoretical length of the side was 230,560 mm.
>
> The length of 524 mm for the cubit of the Pyramid has been confirmed by the endless measurements that have been applied to every detail.'[7]

The range of opinions is within a fraction of a millimetre and we are happy to take Stecchini's highly authoritative opinion and consider the Egyptian royal cubit as being 52.4 centimetres. It did not take us long to arrive at our first assumption that this cubit did not appear to have

[7] http://www.metrum.org/measures/dimensions.htm

any direct connection with either the Sumerian or Megalithic systems.

We then turned to another Ancient Egyptian unit closely related to the royal cubit called the 'remen'. The remen had a relationship with the royal cubit in that if a square had sides of one royal cubit the diagonal from opposite corners will be one remen.

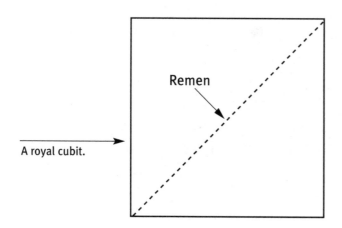

This Ancient Egyptian relationship between two major units of length uses the geometric principle supposedly invented 1,500 years later by Pythagoras, who is credited with observing that 'the square of the hypotenuse of a right-angled triangle is equal to the sum of the squares of the other two sides'.

A simple example of this principle is the classic 3,4,5 triangle. If the triangle has a 3-inch base, a 4-inch high side and a sloping side of 5 inches, and we create a square on each side, the result is three squares of 9, 16 and 25 square inches. Adding the first two together gives 25 square inches, which is equal to the third side. The attribution of this very ancient principle to Pythagoras appears to be another case of the Greeks unwittingly reinventing old knowledge.

It is now accepted that this geometric principle was also important to the Babylonians (and possibly therefore the Sumerians).

THE ORIGIN OF PYTHAGORAS' THEORUM

The basis of this so-called Pythagorean relationship is actually the study of the square root of two. This is because the length of the hypotenuse (the corner-to-corner diagonal) in a square is the square root of the sum of the squares of the other two sides. The Sumerian/Babylonian solution was written down as 1, 24, 51, 10 in their base 60 notation, which would be written today as the decimal number 1.414212963.

If the royal cubit was indeed 52.4 centimetres, then the remen must have been a length equal to 74.1 centimetres. Once again, however, we could find no apparent connection to the Megalithic or Sumerian principles. But we continued to look at the patterns of the cubit/remen relationship. Like the Megalithic people and the Sumerians, the Ancient Egyptians considered halves and doubles to be as valid as the full dimension of most units. The principle of using the side of a square and its hypotenuse lead directly to a sequence of doubling or halving. This can be seen when a series of squares is developed using the hypotenuse.

If the smallest square has sides of a royal cubit, the second square formed on the diagonal will have sides of one remen, and a third square build on the next diagonal will have sides of a double royal cubit. The next obvious step seemed to be to introduce a circle because the Megalithic and Sumerian systems worked with circles.

We could draw an infinite series of squares and circles and they would produce an alternating series of cubit and remen dimensions, doubling as they move outwards, and halving as they go inwards.

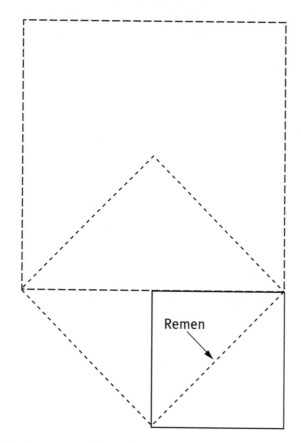

Squares on the hypotenuse of a royal cubit.

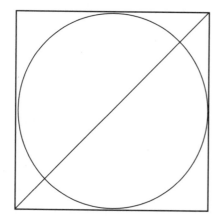

A circle within
a cubit.

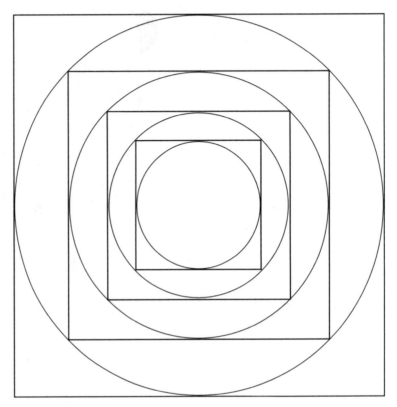

The power of the circle.

All of this was very basic, although it was beautiful and intriguing. Here we had the power of the circle that could be said to define the two major units of Egyptian measurement. The next obvious question was, 'What is the length of circles created by a royal cubit and remen series?' The answer was very interesting.

Taking a square with sides of one quarter-remen (18.526 centimetres) we find that the circle that encloses it is very close indeed to a Megalithic Yard in circumference! At 82.31 centimetres it was 99.2 percent of Thom's Megalithic Yard found in the British Isles. The next square has sides of a half-cubit and the next one a half-remen; the circle that encompasses this square is two Megalithic Yards in circumference.

There is a small discrepancy between the quarter-remen square and the Megalithic Yard circle around it, but we had to remember that a pendulum swing is inversely proportional to gravity, which reduces towards the equator and causes a pendulum with the same period for its swing to be shorter in length. This boils down to the fact that anyone following the rules for a Megalithic Yard would get a noticeably smaller result at the latitude of the pyramids than they would in Orkney, for instance. Alexander Thom's Megalithic Yard was an average derived from all of his measurements taken from Megalithic sites from northern Scotland down to Brittany, and the vast majority were derived from northerly sites. Our conclusion is that the tiny variances in the available data are greater than the inaccuracy found in the principle of the royal cubit and the remen defined by a Megalithic pendulum.

A Megalithic Yard made in Egypt according to the Megalithic pendulum method would be 82.7 centimetres long. This shows that the pendulum method of reproduction must originally have been intended to work only in and around the British Isles. At this southern latitude the same process does not produce a correct geodetic unit. However, for the theoretical Egyptian Megalithic Yard to be the circle in the remen/cubit series the royal cubit would have to be 52.648 centimetres – less than half a percent larger than Stecchini's estimate.

When our manuscript was being checked for scientific accuracy by Peter Harwood, he had been very surprised and eventually impressed with our findings. Peter was doing a great job for us, pointing out some errors in our calculations and drawing our attention to issues we had missed. When he read this section on the possible use of the Megalithic Yard to define the royal cubit he suggested that we appeared to have *inferred* a significant discovery about the Khufu pyramid that we had missed in fact. He reminded us of John Taylor's book *The Great Pyramid*, written in 1859, where it is observed that if one divides the height of the pyramid into twice the size of its base, the result is pi. While some people believed this demonstrated that the ratio we now call pi, must have been sacred to the Egyptians, others had a more prosaic explanation.

Critics of the 'sacred pi' theory pointed out that if a wheel had been made with a diameter that was a subdivision of the height, and it was used to roll out a certain number of revolutions along the sides, the height and sides would automatically have a pi relationship without the builders even realizing it.

Peter Harwood's email went on to say:

'If you have a wheel a foot in diameter, say, then construct a pyramid by making each side of the base square exactly one roll of the wheel long, and the height two diameters of the wheel, you have your pi ratio without actually knowing what pi is. But supposing instead of a foot you use a half cubit diameter wheel. You will end up with a copy of the great pyramid 1 cubit high, with the length of each base side 1 MY! Now that made my pulse race. I can't believe you'd miss such a sexy result.'

Peter was quite right; we had missed a very significant point. The use of a Megalithic-Yard wheel would explain a very old mystery. We checked out the height of the pyramid and found that it is estimated to be 146.59 metres and the sides are estimated to be 230.56 metres. Because all of the estimates of the royal cubit vary a tiny amount we decided to standardize and make the assumption that the Megalithic Yard principle, used in Egypt, had been the starting point. So, taking a Megalithic Yard as 82.7 centimetres and a half royal cubit as 26.324 centimetres, we found the following for the Great Pyramid of Khufu at Giza:

height	= 279 royal cubits
side of base	= 279 Megalithic Yards
corner to corner	= 279 remens

All of the measuring units appeared in the same number when used in Khufu's pyramid. We could only assume that some kind of ancient numerology had made the value '279' deeply meaningful to the architects. Checking other pyramids we found they all appear to have been made to differing requirements, although the other two pyramids at Giza had perimeters that appear to have been measured in Egyptian Megalithic Yards:

Menkaure pyramid (all sides)	= 500 MY
Sahure pyramid (all sides)	= 380 MY

Could it be that the Ancient Egyptians created their own units by using the same 'sacred' principle as the world's first workers in stone? They must have known that there is no other way to create a repeatable unit of measure other than to calibrate the spin of the Earth using the apparent motion of Venus or the stars – and the Egyptians were unquestionably fascinated by the heavens. Their use of Venus and stars in hieroglyphs shows how central they were to the priesthood.

The priests of Ra, the Sun god, may have sought an extra layer of encryption to hide the secrets of the master mason from the common man. One can imagine how they considered the length of the pendulum to be the circumference of the sun and then put a square around it. They would here be using the known Egyptian principle of 'As above – so below' as well as the 'Russian Doll' principle that was central to many early cultures, including that of the Megalithic builders. This meant that the same geometric principle would give them an

The hieroglyph for Venus, which literally means 'Divine Star'

The hieroglyph for the priesthood, showing Venus above the sun

infinite sequence of $1/2$ MY, 1 MY, 2 MY to reveal multiples of royal cubits and remens.

We checked on whether there were any further grounds to believe that the Egyptians had used the principles of the Megalithic measuring system to create their own units. We found them.

In the Egyptian numbering system the circle was used as a hieroglyph to denote the fraction one quarter. In the sequence of circles within squares, the square that contains the circle with a circumference of a Megalithic Yard has sides that measure one quarter-remen. Furthermore, the Ancient Egyptians had a principle unit of area they called the 'setat' (later known to the Greeks as the 'arouna'). This was most commonly used in its quarter form. We were amazed to find that the area of a setat is exactly 4,000 MY^2 and the quarter-setat is therefore precisely 1,000 MY^2. The chances of this being a coincidence are infinitesimally small.

The theory that there was interaction between the Megalithic builders of the British Isles and the Ancient Egyptians was starting to look extremely probable. It has already been noted by other researchers that the inner edge of the circle, or Sarsen Ring, at Stonehenge in southern England has a diameter of 1162.8 inches (2953.51 centimetres), which means that it has an area exactly equal to an Egyptian quarter-setat. Could the Egyptians also have adopted their units of area from the Neolithic people of Britain?

It appears that the early Egyptians were strongly influenced by the Megalithic builders of the British Isles. Such connections have been mooted before but have been rejected by mainstream archaeology because of the absence of cross-cultural artefacts at archaeological dig sites. The assumption that ancient cultures could not have had contact unless they left evidence appears to be unwarranted. The movement of a small number of master mason/magi priests between the British Isles and the Nile Delta could not reasonably be expected to show any trace of artefacts. The discovery of these interrelated measurement principles is far more conclusive evidence of a deep level of influence of one people on another than the digging up of Megalithic objects in the sands of Egypt.

Hidden within the working practices of all Egyptian mathematicians and builders the Megalithic Yard had been present, probably from the very start of the civilization. Megalithic 'DNA' in so significant a place as this surely points to the Egyptian system of measurements also possessing strong traces of the Great Underlying Principle – whatever its origin.

Stonehenge Area

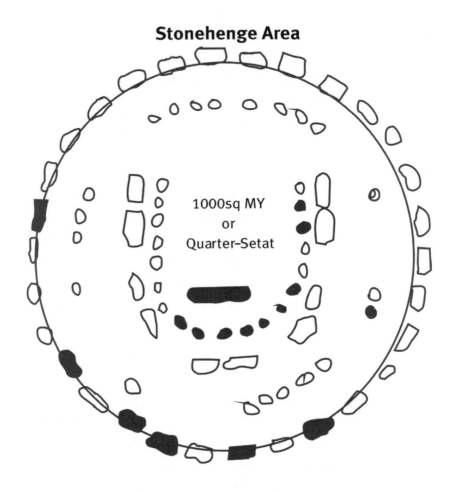

1000sq MY
or
Quarter-Setat

The plan of Stonehenge is designed on an area of a quarter Egyptian setat.

CONCLUSIONS

◎ Many leading linguists accept that there was a single global language approximately 15,000 years ago. Our findings are showing that many cultures shared an approach to measurement and geometry that comes from an apparently single source more than 5,000 years ago.

◎ The Indus Valley civilization or Harappa culture of the Indian subcontinent dating from about 2800 BC had a unit of length called the gaz that is very close indeed to the Megalithic Yard. We dismissed this as a probable coincidence until we became aware of the cube-shaped stone weights that this culture used. These weights correspond almost perfectly to the imperial system. The largest weight weighed 3 pounds and one of the smallest weighed just one four-hundredth of a pound. This was especially interesting as we had already identified that the pound weight is derived from a cube with sides of one-tenth of a Megalithic Yard (4 Megalithic Inches).

◎ The Spanish vara is very close to being a Megalithic Yard as is the old Japanese measure known as the shaku. This is believed to have been imported from China more than 1,000 years ago and is almost indistinguishable from a Minoan foot. It follows, therefore, that 366 Megalithic Yards is the almost the same as 1,000 Japanese shaku, with a fit accuracy of 99.8 percent.

◎ Looking at Ancient Egypt, we noted that the basic unit of linear measurement, in use for nearly the whole of its history was the royal cubit. A related unit of length was the remen which had a Pythagorean relationship to the cubit. This was based on the square root of 2, which the Sumerians/Babylonians wrote down as 1, 24, 51, 10 (in their base 60 notation) but would be written today as the decimal number 1.414212963.

◎ We found that the Great Pyramid of Khufu was built using a measuring wheel with a circumference of one Megalithic Yard and a diameter of a half royal cubit. All of the pyramids main dimensions are a combination of Megalithic Yards, royal cubits and remens, all to the value of '279'.

◎ The Ancient Egyptians also had a principal unit of area called the setat that was most commonly used in its quarter form. The area of a setat is exactly 4,000 MY^2 and the quarter-setat is therefore precisely 1,000 MY^2. The chances of this being a coincidence are minutely small. Further, it has already been noted by other researchers that the inner edge of the circle, or Sarsen Ring, at Stonehenge in southern England has a diameter of 1,162.8 inches, which means that it has an area exactly equal to an Egyptian quarter-setat.

CHAPTER 11

Music and Light

We had found that Megalithic 'DNA' is present in measurement systems spanning a broad period from the Sumerians and Ancient Egyptians through to those devised at the end of the 18th century. The first cultures to compile records of their civilizations have made it relatively easy to understand much about their lives and knowledge but the Megalithic builders left us little to puzzle over except their magnificent structures.

Generations of investigators have assumed that stone circles and other prehistoric monuments were built for some unknown pagan ritualistic purposes by otherwise unsophisticated Stone Age tribes. People with a more romantic bent have sometimes confused matters by speculating on what little is known of the much later Celtic peoples and attributing all kinds of inappropriate magic and mystery to the Megalithic monuments. These romanticists assume that great wisdom was held, almost instinctively, within the minds of a lost cult of nature worshippers. The evidence of Thom's Megalithic Yard has demolished any notion of the naivety of its creators assumed by most arch-aeologists. We have to respect these forgotten people for the great astronomers and geometricians they certainly were.

The level of science achieved by the Sumerians, the Ancient

Egyptians and the Greeks is well understood, but the knowledge of the Megalithic builders of the area around the British Isles can only be reconstructed from a forensic investigation of their artefacts. Sadly, we can never know what myths and legends they handed on down the generations and we will never hear the music they played or the songs they sang.

Further accomplishments of the Megalithic people

As we have seen, however, it is entirely possible to reconstruct the mathematics these people understood and used, and this in turn might just give us some clues as to their other accomplishments. We have established that the number 366 was central to the Megalithic system because it is the number of Earth revolutions in a single orbit around the Sun (a year) and because one 366th part of a day is the difference between a solar and a sidereal day. The second important number in the system was 360, which was the number of seconds in a Megalithic Degree. Megalithic geometry works on a combination of these two numbers.

Alexander Thom had observed that those who built the stone circles and other monuments he studied seemed to have understood the concept that we call pi, the ratio of the diameter of a circle to its circumference. The length of the diameter of a circle fits approximately three and one-seventh times into its circumference. To be more exact we can express the number as 3.14159265, although the string of digits after the decimal point appears to be infinite.

Thom described how some stone rings were made up of carefully calculated parabolas that appeared to be designed to have a ratio of 3:1, instead of pi, for their principal diameter. In other cases, the builders of the circles had 'flattened' the sides of circles or had created 'egg shapes' in an apparent attempt to force pi into an integer relationship of 3:1 that it really cannot possess.

In order to explore more fully the long-dead builders' knowledge of such matters, we decided to look closer at the key Megalithic number of 366 to see if it had any relationship with pi. Rather to our surprise, we quickly found a very important link. Imagine the following scenario:

1. A circle with a circumference of 366 Megalithic Yards is constructed.
2. The perimeter of the circle is then divided into half Megalithic Yards, giving 732 units around the circle.
3. The diameter of the circle will therefore be 233 half Megalithic Yards (732 divided by pi).

A surprising fact about such a circle is that it comes just about as close as possible to having both an integer number of units for its circumference and for its diameter. The difference between a truly integer circumference and diameter in this case is one five-thousandth of a millimetre, across a circle with a circumference of over 260 metres. This tiny fraction is far less than the human eye can discern. To any mathematician from the algorithmic school, this would constitute a perfect fit for all real-world purposes.

We found it fascinating that these Megalithic numbers could produce such near-perfect integer numbers for the circumference and diameter of a circle. So is this resulting diameter of 233 special in any way?

The Fibonacci Series

The answer is that it is very special indeed. While the Greek letter pi is used to denote the ratio of the diameter of a circle to its circumference, the letter 'phi' is used to denote the ratio found in a number sequence known as the Fibonacci Series. Leonardo Pisano Fibonacci

(1170–1250) studied the mating patterns of rabbits and almost accidentally discovered the amazing ratio we now know as phi. The series is where each ascending number is equal to the value of the proceeding two numbers added together: 1, 1, 2, 3, 5, 8, 13, 21, 34, 55, 89, 144, 233, etc. The sequence quickly settles down to the ratio scientists call phi, which is 1.618033989.

Phi is phenomenally important because it is the ratio associated with growth. From flowers to human embryos and from seashells to galaxies – everything in the universe that grows expands outwards according to this fundamental rhythm. The Fibonacci Series was known to the Greeks and to many other early cultures, though it was Finonacci himself who first studied the ratio in a scientific sense. In the fine arts the Series is often referred to as the 'golden section' or the 'golden mean' where it is usually expressed as a 5:8 relationship. The analysis of many Renaissance paintings will show how rigorously this principle was applied. Artists such as Leonardo Da Vinci and Michelangelo for example, would have learned about the golden mean as apprentices and used the principle in almost all their later artistic creations.

The Fibonaccian number of 233 from our 732 circle is composed of the numbers 89 and 144 added together. However, we had to face the possibility that the number 233 turning up in a Megalithic context was simply another coincidence and we certainly felt that we had to investigate the matter further. Then we noticed something rather peculiar when we brought the two irrational ratios of pi and phi together. Multiplying these numbers leads to another unimpressive looking number:

$$3.14159265 \times 1.618033989 = 5.08320369$$

But if we divide our circle of 732 half Megalithic Yards by pi x phi we get an almost perfect result of 144. And this is the number before 233 in the Fibonacci series and again it is an incredibly accurate result. However, this is only a cross-proof of the first observation that a circumference of 732 half Megalithic Yards will produce virtually perfect Fibonaccian results for its diameter. We did find it very odd that the following is true to an astonishing degree of accuracy:

360 divided by 5　　　　 = 72

366 divided by (pi x phi)　= 72

It appears that there is a curious property of the numbers used by the Megalithic people that makes pi and phi work together to define the difference between 360 and 366. The tiny discrepancy in the mathematics described here is just one part in 400,000 – far beyond any engineering tolerance. By some mechanism we still do not understand, it appears that the Megalithic builders were in touch with nature and reality in a way that modern science is yet to achieve. We have extrapolated this relationship from Megalithic principles, but one question we had to ask ourselves was, 'Is there any evidence to suggest that the Megalithic builders *knew* about this mathematical principle made famous in the 13th century by Leonardo Fibonacci?' Our research had produced results that appeared to confirm their awareness of phi and our own observations were bolstered by the totally independent discoveries of Mona Phillips from Ohio. In the 1970s Dr Phillips had looked at Thom's original data from Megalithic sites as a central part of her PhD thesis. She too identified the existence of phi within the Megalithic structures and she contacted Professor Thom, asking that he check her findings. Thom reported back that her results were indeed correct and he said that he found her observations to be quite amazing, calling them, 'almost magical'.

We are sure that Dr Phillips and Professor Thom are correct in suggesting that some Megalithic sites do exhibit the ratio of phi. But did the builders deliberately use it or was it simply a natural consequence of using the number 366 in the building of circles? We had to face the possibility that phi may be simply somehow inherent to the manipulation of the number 366, which appears to have all kinds of 'magical' properties.

We had some difficulty in imagining Neolithic people working with phi, but we decided to investigate other areas where there might be examples of the number 366, in conjunction with the Megalithic Yard, producing results that resonate with nature. After considering a few ideas we elected to look closely at the subject where mathematics meets art – music.

Mathematics meets art

Scientific interest in music goes back a long way. Pythagoras, the Greek remembered primarily for Pythagoras' Theorem, lived between 569 BC and 475 BC and spent years experimenting with music. He is credited with being one of the first individuals to produce a really harmonious musical scale. Pythagoras experimented with stringed instruments to see which notes sounded better when played together. By way of an ingenious system of what are known as 'musical fifths', he worked out how to tune any instrument to produce good harmony. He knew that string length was very important and dealt with music as an exercise in mathematics.

As ever, it seems that the Greeks were great re-inventors of already ancient knowledge and it is now accepted that Pythagoras was far from being the first to carry out such experiments. Sumerian texts indicate that scholars from the culture understood musical scales and tuned by fifths long before the Greek nation came into existence. We are particularly indebted to Fred Cameron, a Californian computer expert with a background in astronomy, who has spent years reconstructing Sumerian scales and then composing music that may be tantalizingly close to the original.

It seemed reasonable to assume that as the Sumerians had sophisticated music, the Megalithic people probably did as well. With this thought in mind we decided to take a completely new approach by returning to the basics of Megalithic mathematics, particularly the half Megalithic Yard pendulum, not just in terms of its linear length, but also with regard to its frequency. It was not long before we found ourselves being drawn into the fascinating world of sound and light.

It would not be possible to perform practically but if we theoretically fastened a pen to the bottom of a Megalithic pendulum and allowed it to swing freely while moving a piece of paper underneath it, we would end up drawing a sine wave (see below).

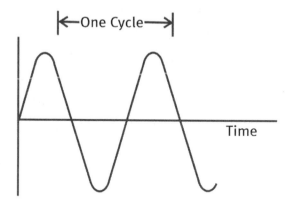

A typical wave showing frequency and length.

The pendulum 'wavelength' is the distance between two peaks or troughs on the sine wave and this would depend on how fast we moved the paper under the pendulum. 'Frequency' is the number of peaks and troughs over a given period of time.

Today we measure frequency in cycles per second, known as hertz, usually shortened to Hz. A simple example is a child banging a toy drum where a rhythm of one bang every second creates a frequency of precisely 1 Hz. If the child doubles the rhythm to two beats per second the frequency would be 2 Hz, and so on. The human ear can detect frequencies up to an amazing 20,000 Hz.

When we hear a note played on a musical instrument, both frequency and wavelength are involved in what our ear registers. The note we choose to call 'A' on a modern piano keyboard, three notes below middle C, has a frequency of 440 Hz, which means there are 440 peaks and 440 troughs, of the sort shown in the diagram above, for every second of time. The note A also produces a wavelength, which in this case is 78.4 centimetres. The next note up on the piano keyboard, B flat, has a frequency of 466.16 Hz and a wavelength of 74 centimetres. As the frequency increases, the wavelength decreases.

We had previously discovered that the modern second of time (plus its double counterpart) was first used by the Sumerians, but we could equally well adopt Megalithic units of distance and time to specify musical notes in exactly the same way.

The Earth turns once every sidereal day of 86,164 seconds and according to Megalithic geometry the equator can be divided into 366 degrees, 60 minutes and 6 seconds of arc. Because the planet bulges a little at the equator its equatorial circumference is larger than the polar circumference and therefore the distance of one second of arc is longer, at just under 366.6 Megalithic Yards. It follows that the Earth will rotate through one Megalithic second of arc every 0.65394657 seconds – which is a period that we might reasonably call a 'Megalithic Second of time'. Therefore, if we had a musical note with a frequency of 366 cycles for every Megalithic Second of time, it would be 'in tune' with the turning Earth because there would be one vibration for every

Megalithic Yard of planetary turn at the equator. In reality it is very slightly more than a Megalithic Yard because of the equatorial bulge. The difference between the polar and equatorial circumferences is equivalent to 36.6 Megalithic Minutes of the polar circumference! We decided to call this theoretical unit of Megalithic sound a 'Thom' (abbreviated to Th) in honour of Alexander Thom whose work is at the root of our investigation. In standard terms, a frequency of 366 Th would be 560 Hz, which places our Megalithic note slightly above C sharp in modern concert tuning.

Once we had our primary note, it would then be possible to tune an entire instrument, or even an entire orchestra, to that note. Since all the notes in a scale are harmonious and therefore have a mathematical relationship with the starting or 'root' note, and because the Megalithic Yard is geodetic, it would follow that any piece of music played in this Megalithic C sharp would enjoy a mathematical relationship with the turning Earth, both in terms of the planet's dimensions and its spin.

The heartbeat of Earth

Alan, a keen musician, began building a series of musical instruments tuned to this Megalithic root note. In particular he decided to create a Megalithic C sharp didgeridoo, the native Australian instrument which is basically just a long, fairly wide tube varying between three and eight feet in length. The didgeridoo is essentially a low-pitched drone-pipe where the player maintains the drone using circular breathing. Originally they were made from straight eucalyptus branches that had been hollowed out by termites but as Alan did not have access to either eucalyptus branches or termites, he used bamboo instead. The exercise worked very well indeed and the resulting sound had a very authentic feel to it so Alan created a second didgeridoo to give to Chris.

Chris had been to Australia, where he had noted a number of

ancient Aboriginal myths for his research when writing *Uriel's Machine*. It is known that some of these myths are 10,000 years old – nearly twice as old as Sumerian stories. Chris suggested that we should try and find out if this particular 'Megalithic' didgeridoo really existed amongst the aborigines and was surprised when Alan replied that he had a good friend who was an authority on the subject. Gordon Hookey, an indigenous Australian, had stayed at Alan's house for a number of weeks when he was visiting Britain to give talks on Aboriginal art and music. Unfortunately, every attempt to contact Hookey for research purposes failed, as he appeared to be permanently on the move. By a quirk of fate, at almost exactly the same time as Alan had given up hope of tracking down his friend the doorbell rang and one of those magical moments of beautiful serendipity occurred. As Alan opened the door a beaming stranger introduced himself saying that he had come to borrow the key to the local Civic Centre, held by Alan and his wife. As the conversation developed Alan was soon open-mouthed.

'I'll come and open up the Centre for you with pleasure. Are you running some course or other?' asked Alan.

'Yes. I'm just beginning a music course with a difference – I teach the didgeridoo.'

'What?!'

Alan stopped in his tracks, staring at the stranger in disbelief.

'I know it sounds pretty weird but it's actually a fascinating subject,' replied the stranger in self-defence.

'No, no, I don't think it's strange at all. It's just that I can't believe that you have turned up on my doorstep at this precise moment in time,' Alan said, shaking his head from side to side in disbelief.

The visitor was carrying a long bag, which he then told Alan contained a number of authentic didgeridoos. It transpired that he had spent considerable periods living in the Australian bush with Aborigines. There he had manufactured his own instruments and had ultimately become one of Britain's few non-Aboriginal experts on the subject. Alan dived right in with the $64,000 question.

'You wouldn't happen to know if native Australians ever use a didgeridoo that produces a note a little over C sharp, would you?'

The reply stunned Alan.

'Something a little over C sharp?'

Hookey paused momentarily as he thought.

'Yes, they certainly do – it's considered to be the most sacred of all tunings and is reserved for playing music to the Earth.'

'Playing music to the Earth!' Alan shouted back at the surprised stranger. 'That's incredible. When you say 'Earth' – do you mean the ground or the entire planet?'

'It's the same thing to native Australians. The note from that didgeridoo harmonizes them to every aspect of their environment. The sound it makes thanks the world for all it gives them and playing it binds them to all of nature. It's a kind of prayer of thanks offered up the planet and, at the same time, the music they make merges them into the whole of creation.'

This was incredible information. It had been a long shot that such an instrument existed at all, but to find out that the Australian Aborigines used an 'Earth' note with a frequency of 366 Th was simply wonderful. One again it could be a huge coincidence and it seemed completely impossible that there would be any calculated connection with Megalithic mathematical principles.

The only reasonable explanation we could come up with was that the note was produced naturally by means of some sort of instinctive harmony between the Australian Aborigines and the revolving planet. Native Australians have a deep spiritual relationship with their environment and their mind-set is completely different to that of the westernized world. This is a race that was cut off from the rest of world more than 40,000 years ago and which has found it hard to come to terms with the materialism of the Europeans that arrived on their remote shores a mere 200 years ago. The Australian government has now realized that it cannot, and maybe should not, necessarily assimilate indigenous Australians into modern lifestyles and so has returned land to the tribes so that they can live in their traditional manner if they so desire.

If we are right in thinking that Aboriginal Australians instinctively understand that the Earth resonates to a note of 366 Th, it follows that there must be some kind of physical reality to the Megalithic geometric divisions of the planet. This indicated that the utterly brilliant system of the Earth breaking down into 366 degrees, 60 minutes and 6 seconds of arc – each a whisker over 366 Megalithic Yards – was much more 'authentic' than we ever imagined. To test this 'intuition' theory we began to cast around the world, trying to find recordings of indigenous music that have not been affected by the specific requirements of Western music or what is now known as concert tuning.

We were trying to find out if there was a common usage of musical pieces set in the key that we called 'Megalithic C', otherwise known as C sharp in the concert scale. In addition, we were looking for specific rhythm patterns that also fell within expected Megalithic parameters. In particular, we were seeking a rhythm of 91.5 beats per modern minute, because 91.5 beats in a modern minute means that every beat is exactly 1 Megalithic Second apart.

From the rainforest of the Andes, the windswept mountains of Tibet, and the frozen wastes of Siberia to the rolling plains of North America, we recognized traces of ethnic music that corresponded with the 'beat of the Earth' almost everywhere we looked. We found it in traditional Indian music, and among the indigenous peoples of Africa. It seemed that wherever a culture was spontaneously creating music, freed from the constraints of the recording studio and standard concert tuning, Megalithic notes and rhythms were once common (see Appendix 4).

We began to accept that Megalithic tunings and rhythms were probably part of the 'heartbeat' of the planet and that human beings are somehow locked into an instinctive knowledge of the fact. Certainly, we could not find Megalithic notes or rhythms in the animal world, only in music created by our own species. As a passing thought it struck us that it might not be entirely coincidental that a normal human heart beats precisely in a range from once per Sumerian second to once per Megalithic Second (a pulse rate of 60 to 91.5 beats per minute).

Sound and light

In its preference for pigeonholing every subject, modern sciences such as medicine and psychology seem to sometimes underestimate the linkage between our species and the Earth. We less live on the planet than we *are* the planet. Just because we have an intellect that gives us a sense of the individual should not hide the fact that we are made of

Earth dust and assembled according to the dynamic qualities that govern our world. With this thought in mind we decided to look at other human senses – especially sight. The light we see is not dissimilar to sound in that it consists of extremely fast oscillations of an electromagnetic field in a particular range of frequencies that can be detected by the human eye. Different colour sensations are produced by light vibrating at different frequencies, ranging from about 4×10^{14} vibrations per second for red light to about 7.5×10^{14} for violet light. The visible spectrum of light is usually defined by its wavelength, ranging from the smallest visible wavelength for violet, at about forty-millionths of a centimetre to seventy-five millionths of a centimetre for red.

We would upset most scientists if we were to suggest that sound has anything to do with electromagnetic radiation, although some 'maverick' academics have made claims that there is a definite relationship. One of these is Dr Jacques Benveniste, former Director at the Institute National de la Santé et de la Recherche Médicale in France. He is quite convinced that audible sounds have a tangible relationship with biological processes, the molecules of which vibrate at a fantastic rate. Unfortunately, Jacques Benveniste is presently 'out in the cold' academically speaking, so his discoveries carry little weight in orthodox circles.

Generally speaking, stars and other objects in space are the source of electromagnetic radiation which, travelling across space at the speed of light, constantly bombard our planet. Much of the electromagnetic radiation falling upon us could be harmful to life and some of it, such as ultraviolet light, is filtered out by our friendly atmosphere.

We use non-visible electromagnetic radiation all the time. Devices

[1] http://twm.co.nz/Benv_bio.htm

such as microwaves and cellular phones, electric fires, radar, radio and television signals, all employ electromagnetic radiation and could not function without it. It is within a narrow section of this very broad spectrum that we find visible light. We are able to 'see' things in the real world because our eyes have become adapted to accepting a very small section of the electromagnetic spectrum and translating it, via our brain, into the sensation we call sight. Where a particular colour is reflected from an object, for example green from most foliage, it passes into our eyes, where the specific frequency and wavelength are recognized and translated, with the aid of memory, into what we 'know' as green.

Unlike electromagnetic radiation, sound cannot exist in the vacuum of space because it is simply a disturbance in the medium in which it travels. Since it relies on the atmosphere, or some other medium, sound has a very much lower speed than light. But because the electromagnetic spectrum has frequency and wavelength, as does sound, we use the same unit, the hertz, to measure both sound and light.

Then we discovered, more or less by accident, that the frequency of the basic Megalithic note of 366 Th (560 Hz) has an unusual property. If we double this frequency exactly 40 times, we arrive at $6.15726511 \times 10^{14}$ Hz, which just happens to bring us to the visible spectrum and to that part of it that we see as the colour blue. Even though, from the standpoint of physics, there is no apparent connection between a sound of 560 Hz and an electromagnetic frequency of $6.15726511 \times 10^{14}$ Hz, there has to be a 'sympathetic resonance' between the two. This fact may, in some so far unknown way, be understood by the Aborigine playing his didgeridoo under the bright blue skies of Australia.

The visible part of the electromagnetic spectrum more or less neatly coincides, in fact, 40 octaves up, with one full octave or scale on a musical instrument. It is possible to see the note F as the start of the colour sequence of visible light at the lower end of the infrared band; the sequence continues through all the notes, to E, which is resonant with ultraviolet. Traditionally there are seven colours to light; red, orange, yellow, green, blue, indigo and violet. In reality, there are as many colours as one wishes to name, as each colour changes imperceptibly into the next throughout the visible spectrum. The relationship between any given musical note and its corresponding resonant colour is described in detail in Appendix 4.

It appears quite remarkable that human beings can see almost exactly one 'octave' of colour. Perhaps, to creatures that see in frequencies below or above our capabilities, the colours repeat, as do musical notes. After all, the last colour in the visible spectrum, violet, is well on the way to becoming red, the starting point of visible light for us.

There is no doubt that the note we call Megalithic C (just above C sharp in the international musical scale) has a sympathetic frequency resonance with the colour we know as blue. Before any physicists reading these words begin to jump up and down with rage at the liberties we appear to be taking here, let us state again that we are not suggesting a 'direct' relationship between sound and light, rather the possibility of a subtle harmony when viewed from a human perspective.

Nobody fully understands the way the human brain deals with information relating to sound or light once the necessary signals have been created by the auditory and optic nerves. It seems very probable that both types of signal are processed, deep within the brain in more or less the same way. We know this must be the case because of a mysterious and sometimes debilitating medical condition known as synesthesia. This is an involuntary process in which one sensory experience is accompanied by another. It takes many forms, but probably the most common is that in which the sufferer genuinely 'sees' a colour upon hearing a particular sound. This condition is well documented and has been studied extensively. The best explanation for its cause is some sort of involuntary crossover within the complex circuitry of the brain, though the latter is an unbelievably complex organ and the process involved is not understood in detail. It was thinking about this bizarre condition that made us consider a real link between the frequency of sound and that of light. It has been a long journey from the simple, single-celled creatures that started life on Earth to the complex structure that is a human being today, and on that long road of evolution we have gradually accumulated the senses we now enjoy. Light sensitivity may have been one of the first of the senses to develop and, ultimately, it did so within a very narrow band of the electromagnetic spectrum. If, as many believe, sensitivity to sound came later, it would surely not be too peculiar for a developing nervous system to concentrate on sounds that had frequencies with a sympathetic resonance to the light frequencies it had already learned to interpret. This might go some way to explaining the occurrence of synesthesia.

If both of these frequency ranges of sound and light should also be inextricably tied to the natural matrix of cycles present in our little world, we surely could not be too surprised. After all, we are part of it.

Megalithic C and water

Interpreting the information in this manner shows that Megalithic C is related, in terms of resonance, with the colour blue. It is interesting to note that the majority of the colour blue visible on our planet is represented by our vast oceans. Many people assume that the seas of the world are blue simply as a result of reflection from the sky which, in a cloudless condition is also blue. This is not the case. The sky is blue because of particles in the atmosphere which react in a rather strange way and which, through a process known as Rayleigh Scattering, give a cloudless sky its colour. But even if the water in our oceans did not reflect the colour of the sky, it would still be blue. We think of water as being colourless, but in reality, it is not. In a laboratory in Kamioka, Japan, there is an indoor pool of absolutely pure water which stands under a silver roof. The water in the pool is a deep and luxuriant shade of blue.

Water is the absolute basis of all life on Earth and, as far as is known, life cannot exist in an environment in which no water is present. Being composed of two hydrogen atoms to one oxygen atom (H_2O), water remains one of the most mysterious and intriguing molecules known.

We suspect, but at the moment cannot prove, that the sympathetic frequency relationship between the fundamental Megalithic C and that of the colour blue may in some way be related to our utter dependence on water and the way we have evolved to take account of that reliance.

All of the above leads us to suspect that there is probably far more to the linear length we call the Megalithic Yard than at first seemed to be the case. So neatly does this unit fit into the matrix of the turning Earth, and into patterns we have evolved to utilize and appreciate it, its importance may prove to be pivotal to our very survival.

It is almost certain that the Megalithic Yard is a physical manifestation of patterns that are inextricably linked to our life on this planet. Despite this fact, its length cannot be ascertained instinctively but has to be produced through a mechanical means (i.e. a pendulum). That any supposedly primitive culture was able to draw it forth from the complex interactions of nature in the way that the Megalithic people did is little short of staggering.

Postscript

After we had finished writing this book we decided that it would be fascinating to lay out the detailed rules of Megalithic music that we had just reconstructed. We then asked a young London-based band called De Lorean to respond to a brief to create modern music that carefully followed the ancient principles of sound that are associated with the Megalithic Yard.

Jim Evans, Adam Falkus, Paul Newton and Will Skidmore, who are all highly talented musicians, took the brief and went very quiet for many weeks. Then they came back with their first track 'Heliotropic'. It was electrifying!

Over the following months they went on to write and perform many other pieces that interpreted the Megalithic rules in a variety of ways, creating music that seemed to us to synchronize with the soul. As we listened we felt in tune with the power of the turning Earth.

Those readers who would like to hear samples of De Lorean's music, or buy the full CD entitled *Civilization One – The Album* should visit our website at www.civilizationone.com.

CONCLUSIONS

◎ We found that the Megalithic numbers produced circles that combined the mathematical ratios known pi and phi. Both are irrational numbers yet they produced results that are so close to being perfect to be negligible. In our investigation we found that an American PhD student had discovered the existence of phi in Thom's data back in the early 1970s – a fact confirmed by the great man himself when he described the finding as 'magical'.

◎ The all-important numbers 366 and 360 are curiously linked by a combination of pi and phi because 360 divided by 5 gives a result of 72 and 366 divided by pi x phi also gives the result of 72. This suggests that the relationship between the two Megalithic numbers has a fundamental resonance with these two very special ratios.

◎ When we turned to the subject of music we found that Megalithic mathematics produces its own structure. Sound is normally measured in cycles per modern second, known as hertz (Hz), but we considered using cycles per Megalithic Second, which we called Thoms (Th). A frequency of 366 Th is the same as 560 Hz, which places our Megalithic note just slightly above C sharp in modern concert tuning. This is effectively the 'sound of the Earth turning' because the planet rotates at a rate of one Megalithic Yard per beat at the equator.

◎ We found that indigenous Australians consider a didgeridoo with a note equal to 366 Th capable of creating sacred Earth music. Further investigation of other indigenous music also revealed Megalithic rhythm and pitch correspondences. It appears that there is an instinctive relationship between the rotating mass of the planet and human music. It may indeed have been this 'involuntary' sense that the mystic and mathematician Pythagoras came to call 'the harmony of the spheres'.

◎ When we looked at human sight we found that the visible part of the electromagnetic spectrum forms an octave rather like music. What is more, if we move exactly 40 octaves up the frequency scale from a note of 366 Th we get to blue light. While nearly all scientists believe that light and sound are not connected, we tentatively feel that there might be a resonance between the two that is picked up by human perception.

CHAPTER 12

Sun, Moon and Megalithic Measure

It was clearly time to sit and take stock again. We had a series of face-to-face meetings in order to review our data and some of the remarkable findings that had resulted from our investigation. We were agreed that we found ourselves faced by certain irreconcilable facts. The association of the numbers 366 and 360 had proved to be far more puzzling than we could have possibly expected. What is more, we were now aware that we were not the first investigators to associate knowledge of both pi and phi with the data Alexander Thom had collected in his long investigations of the Megalithic sites.

The challenge we now faced was to try and understand how Neolithic Man could have devised a unit that was obviously central to a gloriously holistic system of measurement that seems to emanate from the Earth itself. Did they invent it? Was it given to them by some unknown previous but more advanced culture, or does everything come from the human condition, in which simple observation of our environment will intuitively link us to a natural rhythm of 366?

We had constantly tried to stand back to try and understand what sort of 'magic' was driving a system that was in some ways far in advance of the best we have today – yet existing more than 5,000 years ago. We had the feeling that there was far more here than simply good astronomical observation or the fruits of the efforts of a group of early sky watchers who just got outrageously lucky. At each stage we had found that the Great Underlying Principle had astonishing powers of cohesion to make all aspects of life work as one. Its existence had been made clear to us while others had not found it, probably because we did not impose the limitations of our expectations or preferences on the possibilities.

We had uncovered an integration of ancient units that had no right to exist according to standard opinions of the past. The reality of the Minoan foot and its correspondence to the Megalithic Yard indicated a science that was deliberately and intentionally amended to meet new requirements. The Minoan foot is nowhere near the same linear measurement as the Megalithic Yard, yet it was clearly intended that 1,000 Minoan feet should represent the same linear distance as 366 Megalithic Yards, which itself is exactly one Megalithic Second of arc of the polar circumference of the Earth.

Where to start?

But where, we mused, was the start of this puzzle? Where exactly was the entry point for this impossibly brilliant system that made all modern approaches to working with nature look awkward and entirely compromised. Having more or less exhausted our ideas as to where we could turn next, we looked outwards – towards the heavens themselves.

The first object we considered was Earth's companion in space, that rocky body we simply call the Moon. As inhabitants of planet Earth we should all be eternally grateful to the Moon for orbiting our beautiful blue planet in the way it does. Atypically for the solar system at large, Earth's Moon has large dimensions for a planetary satellite but it has a very low mass because it contains almost no iron or other heavy metals. There is no theory of the Moon's origin that fits all the available facts but it is generally accepted that it is composed of the same materials as the Earth though without the heavy elements. This gives it a density that is around 60 percent of our own world.

The Moon is a great deal more than a shining disc that conveniently lights up the night sky. Several leading biologists working with astrophysicists who study our nearest neighbour in space have come to the conclusion that life on Earth may never have established itself at anything more than a primordial aquatic level if the Moon had not been in place.

The Earth has a very active and unstable core and therefore wobbles in several different ways as it spins. It is has been suggested by some scientists that the Moon acts rather like the stabilizer on a child's bicycle, in that its gravitational presence prevents the Earth from regularly toppling over in relation to its solar orbit. If it did so, any complex life form would be wiped out in the resulting turmoil. In addition, the strong gravitational pull of so massive an object creates by far the largest proportion of the tides we experience.

Biologists have argued that it was the regular cycles of the tides that allowed aquatic life to eventually take up residence on land. For example, some species may have occupied an evolutionary niche provided by tidal pools. If such pools are created during a particularly high tide, it may be some days or even weeks before the sea would replenish them. Natural evaporation would eventually remove the water in the pools, leaving their inhabitants either to die – or to adapt. Creatures exploiting this niche would have been subject to evolutionary forces, which eventually led to the formation of primitive organs for breathing in a part-air/part-water environment. Ultimately, these organs would have become lungs, while fins for swimming evolved into proto-limbs. This is a persuasive theory of how life left the oceans and ultimately evolved into humankind.

By some absolutely incomprehensible quirk of nature, the Moon also manages to precisely imitate the movements of the Sun when both are viewed from Earth. Practically every phenomenon of the Moon replicates, in a month, what the Sun appears to do in a full year. In addition, the magic of the Moon causes it to move in a mirror image of the Sun, in that the midsummer full Moon will set at the same angle and in the same place on the horizon as the midwinter sunset. Then the midwinter Moon sets where the midsummer Sun sets, and at the equinoxes the Moon takes the same setting line as the Sun. This is very, very odd – but it is observably true. [1]

The realities of the Moon are highly improbable for many reasons but we accept them because of what is known as the 'Anthropic Principle'. This states that things have to be as they are or we humans would never have developed to witness them – in other words, our environment exists in its current form because we observe it. To us this seems a rather circular argument that appears to be a handy mechanism to stop us from worrying too much about the extreme improbability of the human species existing at all. When one considers the nature of the Moon, it has to be agreed that no-one could have done a better job if they had sat down and thoughtfully designed the thing!

[1] Heath, R.: *Sun, Moon and Earth*. Wooden Books Ltd, London, 2001.

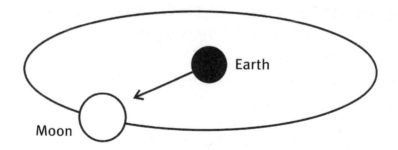

The orbit of the Moon.

The movements of the Moon

We decided to consider the movements of the Moon more closely. Because it always has the same side facing Earth, one lunar day is exactly the same as a rotation around the Earth. This is because the Moon rotates once on its axis as it makes one orbit of the Earth.

The so-called 'dark side' of the Moon is not actually dark, it is simply that one side always faces away from us, like a shot-putter's weight on the end of a line. The Moon orbits the Earth at an average distance of 384,403 kilometres and at an average speed of 3,700 kilometres per hour, and it completes one revolution in an elliptical orbit about the Earth in 27.3217 days. But this is a very human description of events, seen from an Earth-bound perspective. A better way of describing what is happening is to say that the Earth experiences 27.3217 mean solar days for every one of the Moon's days, and this leads to a very surprising outcome:

$$366 \text{ lunar days} = 10,000 \text{ Earth days}$$

Why should this be? This connection by way of the key Megalithic value of 366 is surely no coincidence?

It must also be borne in mind that the number of seconds in a mean solar day (86,400) multiplied by 27.3217 is extraordinarily close

191

to the difference in seconds between 10,000 mean solar days and 10,000 sidereal days. The Moon had always been considered to be improbable – but now it was looking impossible! We were truly stunned as we tried to take in this amazing matrix that stemmed from what we had called the Great Underlying Principle.

An elegant and precise relationship

Our own questions demanded that we try to find an explanation for why the movement of the Moon corresponds to the Megalithic number of 366 so readily. So we looked more closely at the Moon's dimensions and found that its circumference is almost exactly 3.66 times smaller than the Earth's. Then, just for thoroughness, we applied the principles of Megalithic geometry against lunar dimensions.

Earth's Moon is usually quoted as having an equatorial radius of 1738.1 kilometres,[2] giving it a circumference of 10,920,804 metres. This distance seems entirely arbitrary when viewed in metric units but when we converted to Megalithic Yards the principles of the assumed Megalithic geometry are applied and the picture looked staggeringly different.

lunar circumference	=	13,162,900 MY
one lunar Megalithic Degree (366th)	=	35,964 Megalithic Yards
one Lunar Megalithic Minute (60th)	=	599.4 Megalithic Yards
one Lunar Megalithic Second (6th)	=	99.9 Megalithic Yards

[2] http://nssdc.gsfc.nasa.gov/planetary/factsheet/moonfact.html

That is a staggeringly accurate 100 Megalithic Yards to a second of arc!

Allowing for the impossibility of having an entirely accurate estimation of the its circumference, it appears that on the Moon there are 100 MY to a lunar second of arc. For the Megalithic Yard to have a perfect integer fit would only require a tiny adjustment in the assumed radius of the Moon from 1738.1 kilometres to 1739.83 kilometres – a difference that does not exist as the original figure was only intended to be more or less correct to one decimal place.

What was going on? How could there be precisely a hundred Megalithic Yards to a lunar Megalithic Second of arc? It is an inescapable fact that Megalithic geometry works on the Moon as well as the Earth!

Why is it that the Moon conforms so elegantly and precisely to units devised by the Stone Age inhabitants of the British Isles and Brittany? As we thought about the result we could see that the fact that the Earth is 3.66 times larger than the Moon would produce this relationship – but who could have foreseen the astounding level of accuracy. However, it seemed that someone in the distant past had noticed the relationship. All this had to be part of the amazing importance of the number that the Megalithic builders chose as their key value. But, in the light of the lack of sophistication of these people, is it rational to believe that they could possibly have understood all this, or had they simply hit upon some cosmic constant that is unknown in our present era?

The Moon and the Sun

Another strange fact about the Moon is that when viewed from the Earth it appears to be the same size as the Sun. This is why it fits 'exactly' across the disc of the Sun at the time of total solar eclipse. The underlying reason for this is that the Sun is 400 times larger than the Moon but, by yet another amazing quirk of nature it is also 400 times further away from the Earth than the Moon.

The Sun, being 400 times larger than the Moon, means that the following breakdown must apply:

one solar Megalithic   =   14,400,000 Megalithic Yards
   Degree

one solar Megalithic   =   240,000 Megalithic Yards
   Minute

one solar Megalithic   =   40,000 Megalithic Yards
   Second

For thoroughness we decided to check this result against the Sun's radius, which is normally taken as 696,000 kilometres.[3] To find a circumference this has to be doubled and multiplied by pi and then by 1,000 to give a result in metres. This comes out at a very unimpressive 4,373,096,974 metres, but converting it according to the principles of Megalithic geometry does indeed produce a Megalithic Second of arc that is 40,004 Megalithic Yards long. That is one hundredth of one percent different to the estimate of the Sun's dimensions – which is certainly inside the range of error of the original estimate. The best figure of 696,000 kilometres for the radius is obviously rounded up, yet the actual figure we arrive at by using Megalithic principles is 696,070 kilometres. So the Sun also conforms precisely to the Great Underlying Principle. Simply amazing!

The grand design

As we pondered these new revelations we agreed that things like this are not generally encountered in real life but here they were – real, hard

[3] Microsoft® Encarta®, 2003.

facts. The Sun, the Moon and the Earth all conform to a 'grand design' that is also evident in the Megalithic structures that are scattered across the British Isles and western Europe. Is there something absolutely fundamental about the dimensions of the solar system that modern science has missed but which the Stone Age builders understood either intuitively or intellectually?

There is no theory of how the Moon came into being that fits all of the known facts but these days it is widely accepted that the Moon is made of material scooped from the surface of the Earth. This is known as the 'big whack theory' and involves the theoretical catastrophic collision of the Earth with a planet-sized body. This theory also explains why the Moon has virtually no iron because such an impact would have blasted off chunks of the Earth's outer layers rather than its very dense core. If the big whack theory is correct, one could imagine that the debris created might have coalesced in a manner that somehow reflects the same '366-ness' of the Earth, but it seems very strange. As far as we can discover, there is no such effect known to science. Whatever the origin of this orbiting lump of rock, it now becomes clear that the relationships between the Earth, its Moon and the Sun are far more complex and mathematically integrated than anyone in the modern era has realized.

The next step was to look at the dimensions, mass and movements of the other planets in the solar system. We studied each in turn and in every case we found precisely nothing that came anywhere close to fitting the rules of the Megalithic principle. This was reassuring on one level, because it showed that these sorts of numbers and relationships are special. But the consequences of that 'specialness' were worrying. We had to admit that it seems as though humanity's environment has been exclusively engineered for our benefit using a standard measuring system.

A good friend of Chris's, Dr Hilary Newbigin, who is a keen mathematician, suggested that the other planets may have their own value based on their spin to orbit ratio. This could not apply to some planets, such as Venus, which turns the wrong way and has a day slightly longer than its year. However, it could work for other planets such as Mars which would have the 'magic number' 688 to match Earth's 366. But this supposed Martian value does not seem to produce any usable pattern, so it looks as though the Earth was very special in some way.

Although the other planets do not appear to conform to the Sun-Earth-Moon values, there are two of them that are of special importance to our planet in general and humanity in particular.

First, if Jupiter was not the size it is and occupying the position it does, the Earth would be regularly bombarded with comets and other space debris.[4] The gravity of this giant planet draws in and consumes most of these missiles before they impact on Earth, just as it did in July 1994 when comet Shoemaker-Levy 9 smashed into Jupiter, creating a fireball larger than our own planet. Quite simply, no higher species would ever have had sufficient catastrophe-free time to develop upon Earth if Jupiter was not so carefully 'guarding' us.

Then there is Venus. This planet has been worshipped by more cultures than any other in the solar system, mainly because it provides humanity with a calendar that is very accurate across a 40-year cycle. It is certain that the Megalithic builders used Venus to calibrate their lives,[5] and it was used to check timekeeping right up to the invention of atomic clocks half a century ago.

From the start of our research our only real intention had been to either prove or disprove the genuineness of the Megalithic Yard, as

[4] Gribbin, J. and Plagemann, S.: *The Jupiter Effect*. New English Library, London, 1980.
[5] Knight, C. and Lomas, R.: *Uriel's Machine*. Arrow, London, 2000.

rediscovered and named by Professor Alexander Thom. Clearly, things had not stopped there, and now we found ourselves on the receiving end of an avalanche of information and figures that showed exactly how important Thom's 50 years of relentless information-gathering had actually been.

The Megalithic Yard divides into the polar circumference of the Earth equally, into a total of 48,224,160 units. It can further be subdivided into increments of 366 MY for the Megalithic Second of arc, 2,196 MY for the Megalithic Minute of arc and 131,760 for the Megalithic Degree of arc. If the Megalithic Yard is, as Thom suggests, 2.722 statute feet or 82.96656 centimetres, it fits the polar circumference of the Earth as indicated here to an extremely high degree of accuracy. The Megalithic Yard is 'truly' geodetic.

In the world of the Megalithic system, a second of arc of an Earth-turn at the equator is exactly the same thing as a second of time. This makes our modern system look half-baked, where a second of arc at the equator is a little under 31 metres and it takes about 15 seconds of time for the Earth to spin through this distance. Stone Age Man has left us looking pretty stupid when it comes to devising an integrated system of time, geometry and distance!

The Megalithic Yard not only accurately bisects the Earth, it does exactly the same on the Moon and the Sun. In the case of these two bodies, it manages on the way to turn the 366s of the Megalithic system into fully functional decimal integers, with long strings of zeros. So the Megalithic Yard is not only geodetic, it is also 'lunardetic' and 'solardetic' (if we are allowed to invent two new words).

There can be no doubt whatsoever that the Megalithic system of measurement was designed specifically for the Earth, even though it is also applicable to the Sun and the Moon. The beauty of the system is that it works so completely: even the difference between the Earth's polar circumference and its equatorial circumference is equal to 36.6 Megalithic Minutes of distance. This fact alone creates a neat form of trigonometry that makes establishing the circumference of the Earth at any latitude a simple matter. And, we must remember how the Megalithic system produces a unit of weight that is the same as the modern pound. With a unit of mass derived from a 4 Megalithic-Inch cube, it describes the mass of the Earth in Megalithic Seconds of arc with the completely round number of 1,000,000,000,000,000,000,000 pounds to one Megalithic-Second segment.

The Megalithic system was provided with a simple compensation mechanism that keeps the 366-day year in tune with the real solar year. This involves removing 1 day from the calendar every 1 year, 4 months and 4 days (492 days). If this simple procedure is followed, the ritual year and the solar year will stay in harmony for well over 3,000 years without any other compensation being necessary.

So, the Megalithic system deals easily with time, distance, mass and volume in a way that is directly proportional to the size, mass and orbital characteristics of the Earth. It some ways it is superior to the metric system and clearly represents the Great Underlying Principle, since everything that came after it has a relationship to it in one way or another.

Meanwhile, the Sumerian system, though working in a slightly different way, is like the other half of some magnificent original framework that describes the physics of humanity's environment from the speed of light to a kilogram of apples. All measurements in the Sumerian system can be cross-checked with known numbers of barley grains, both in terms of distance and mass, while time can be checked against a pendulum of the basic linear length across one 360th part of turning Earth. The Sumerian system also defines the speed of light as being 600,000,000 kush per Sumerian second. The only apparent shortfall in the Sumerian system is that, unlike the Megalithic system, it is not geodetic.

Our archaeological quest has thrown us headlong into something far, far bigger than we could have ever imagined. It only remained to try and make sense of everything we had found.

CONCLUSIONS

◎ It is suggested that humans would not exist if it were not for the size and mass of the Moon. The Moon has many strange properties including the fact that its risings and settings completely mirror those of the Sun during a year.

◎ We looked at the circumference of the Moon and found that it conforms to Megalithic geometry with precisely 100 Megalithic Yards to a lunar second of arc. Then we found that the Sun also conforms to Megalithic geometry with 40,000 Megalithic Yards to a second of arc. No other bodies of the solar system conform to these principles.

◎ When we looked at the movement of the Moon we found that the Earth experiences 27.3217 days for every one of the Moon's days (which is the same as one lunar orbit of the Earth). While the number 27.3217 sounds entirely arbitrary a quick calculation showed that the Moon makes 366 orbits in just 10,000 Earth days!

◎ A Megalith Second of arc and a second of time were the same thing, and are equal to 366 Megalithic Yards at the equator. This makes our modern, non-integrated system look pathetically unsophisticated.

CHAPTER 13

A New Paradigm of Prehistory

The investigation and its challenge to science

We had set out to investigate a tightly defined question: 'Had Professor Alexander Thom been correct in believing that the Megalithic builders had used a standard unit of 82.96656 centimetres?' We were able to conclude that he was absolutely right by identifying the reason why the unit was important and by replicating the precise technique used to make it.

Having confirmed that Thom's brilliant work was indeed valid, a harmless little follow-up experiment into potential Megalithic units of weight and capacity produced such outrageous results that we quickly found ourselves catapulted into a far broader and more complex investigation. This eventually led us on a strange journey that culminated in the rediscovery of an ancient mathematical matrix that echoes some of the deepest patterns of the solar system.

Scientific theories are ways of explaining the world we see around us and the proof of a theory normally comes from making a prediction that is subsequently demonstrated to be correct. Alexander Thom did not make predictions regarding his Megalithic units but, in identifying them so accurately, he laid the ground for them to be subsequently proven. In addition, the fact that even he accepted that there was then no plausible explanation for how such exact units could exist over such a large area also provides a mechanism to demonstrate that he was correct.

If Thom's Megalithic Yard and the Half Megalithic Yard had been nothing more than phantoms erroneously generated from his huge collection of data, as many archaeologists have suggested, then the lengths concerned should be meaningless. The fact that these precise units define the length of a pendulum that gives 366 beats during Venus' path across one 366th of a day is unlikely to be a random chance event.

The technique of replicating the Megalithic Yard requires only simple tools and minimal astronomical knowledge – and it provides an elegantly simple explanation of how the unit was so consistently accurate across time and space. Each user merely created their own measuring rod by timing the turning of the Earth.

Our initial suspicion that a system of prehistoric geometry based on 366 degrees had been in use for thousands of years and across a large geographical area was confirmed as we looked more closely at known and accepted ancient measuring systems. For there to be exactly 1,000 Minoan feet to the Megalithic Second of arc is as stunning as Thomas Jefferson's observation that a precise 1,000 ounces make up a cubic foot of water. From this and other open-minded observations, America's third president concluded that there must be some ancient intelligence underlying the apparently arbitrary measuring units of his day – and now, so have we.

From the previously available evidence the world had reasonably assumed that humans first invented the crudest form of science and principles of measurement some 5,000 years ago and that we have progressed from rough measures, based on paces or approximate body parts, to our refined modern measures across the intervening millennia. But the evidence put forward in this book turns this worldview on its head.

We have found that the further back in time we go, the greater the interconnection between units – and the deep science behind the very oldest measures makes modern systems seem arbitrary and trivial. It appears that before history was written there was an apparently single approach to measurement units that was based on the physical realities of the Sun, the Moon and the Earth.

Of course, such a description of history is counterintuitive. But it is important to remember that several leading experts studying the development of language have already surprised the academic community by concluding that the thousands of languages across the globe all stemmed from a single proto-language. In effect, the further back in time one looks – the greater the conformity. The intuitive, but incorrect, assumption had always been the reverse – that the spoken word began as thousands of tribal tongues that slowly evolved into regional and then national languages.

If our observations are correct, even in part, then archaeology will have to throw away its old paradigm of the development of civilization and build a new picture that will be very different. Furthermore, modern science will have to accept that there is a great deal to learn about the way our world works by looking closely at this long forgotten Great Underlying Principle.

This will not be easy for the academic community. Archaeology has held out against accepting Alexander Thom's theories by failing to put sufficient energy into confirming or disproving his data and his conclusions. The discipline's collective inaction has allowed archaeology to retain its old views intact – but the evidence put forward in this book is infinitely more simple to understand and to check than Thom's specialist methodology and heavyweight data.

Science is regarded as a process governed by rationality, logic and truth. The scientist is expected to carefully and objectively observe, collect and classify information before formulating a hypothesis in order to explain the data and to predict what might happen under various conditions. All theories are subject to modification or replacement as new knowledge is generated. If it were not so we would all still subscribe to the views of Thales who, in the 6th century BC, described the Earth as a flat disc floating on water that he called 'the universal element'.

The information we have uncovered may be ignored by many, but we feel sure that the principles of science will cause it to be carefully examined by experts from different disciplines. We greatly look forward to others taking our findings and developing a bigger and broader picture of the origins of civilization. We also realize that it may take a little time.

Astronomer Professor Archie Roy once told Chris that academia follows a three-point pattern when new information comes from an 'out-of-discipline' source:

1. First it will suggest you are mad and try to ignore you.
2. Then, when you don't go away, it will say, 'Okay, show me your thesis and I will point out why you are wrong.'
3. Finally it will say, 'Well, yes – of course, we knew that all along.'

We hope that Professor Roy is right.

We are confident of our facts because all of the original input data we have used comes from entirely respectable sources – people who are expert in their own fields. The vast bulk of the data used, from the length of the Minoan foot to the mass of the Earth, is not debated by everyone. The sums we have done are able to be checked by anyone with a calculator and a basic knowledge of mathematics, so the calculations are either right or they are wrong.

If the facts we quote are correct and our maths is not flawed, any debate about our thesis will centre on interpretation. We have been as careful as we can be to only assume a *potential* connection where a numerical fit has been very defined and we have secondary corroborating factors. For example, we have not as yet felt able to include the Japanese shaku or the Spanish vara in our big picture, despite very close fits.

We have soundly rejected the notion of a gigantic string of coincidences. Consider, for instance, Thomas Jefferson's brand new units of length that just happened to have precisely 1,000 such units to 360 Megalithic Yards. His use of the Sumerian second of time for a pendulum inadvertently tied him into the ancient underlying pattern.

'Pattern seekers'

However confident we feel about our findings we must finally make sure that we are not fooling ourselves by creating patterns that do not really exist. Mathematics is certainly an area where 'pattern seekers' can delude themselves.

Indeed, the first reaction of many scientists when they hear of our thesis may well be to assume that we are simply pattern seekers. It is an entirely reasonable assumption before the facts are viewed. So, have we deluded ourselves in this way? Perhaps the best way to judge is to look at a couple of well-known examples of delusional pattern-building.

In 1859 John Taylor wrote a book entitled *The Great Pyramid*, in which he observed that if one divides the height of the pyramid into twice the size of its base, the result is very close to the ratio we call pi. Others later observed that the base of the Great Pyramid divided by the width of a casing stone equals the number of days in the year. And later still, it was discovered that if one multiplies the height of the Great Pyramid to the 109th power, the result is the approximate distance from the Earth to the Sun. Taylor's original point is mathematically close and may or may not have been a deliberate design feature of this single structure. But in our view the other points are simply poppycock. So, there is no pattern here, just a one-off observation without any connection to anything else, for example, the other two pyramids at Giza. This bears no similarity to the systematic fits we have been finding underpinning ancient weights and measures.

Another much-quoted case involved mathematician Martin Gardner, who thought that all pattern seeking is foolishness. He set out to make his point by analysing the Washington Monument to deliberately produce a spurious pattern. He found that the number 5 could be shown to be inherent in the structure as follows:

> The height of the monument is 555 feet and 5 inches while its base is 55 feet square. The windows are set at 500 feet from the base and if the base is multiplied by 60 (5 times the number of months in a year) the result is 3,300, which is the exact weight of the capstone in pounds. In addition, he pointed out that the word 'Washington' has exactly 10 letters (2 x 5). Finally, if the weight of the capstone is multiplied by the size of the base, the number 181,500 is produced – which is just under 3 percent away from being the speed of light in miles per second.

Gardner's pattern was created to demonstrate the futility of making patterns with otherwise meaningless numbers. But he had no mathematical pattern at all. There was no reason for choosing the number 5 and there is no mathematical relationship at all between the area of the base and the height of the Monument. There is no reason for introducing the number of months in a year and it is meaningless to multiply units of weight by units of area to produce a speed measured in miles per second. This 'approximation' to the speed of light is wildly out, even if there were any reason for introducing it in the first place.

We are grateful to Martin Gardner for putting our minds at rest by demonstrating how difficult it is to invent patterns that do not exist.

The astonishing truth

We started out with a working hypothesis that the Earth was divided into 366 degrees, 60 minutes and 6 seconds to produce a second of arc on the Earth's circumference that is 366 Megalithic Yards (and 1,000 Minoan feet). This has produced such a range of fruitful results we believe it has to be accepted as real. We were stunned, and very confused, when we found the same geometric divisions are applied to the Moon and the Sun:

> A lunar second of arc that is 100 Megalithic Yards long

> A solar second of arc that is 40,000 Megalithic Yards long

A good scientific theory is one that makes a prediction that is subsequently proven. These findings were not directly predicted by us but we had predicted that there was a Great Underlying Principle that was a physical reality for our human environment. The circumferences of the Moon and Sun are 10,927 and 4,373,097 kilometres respectively, which are perfectly meaningless numbers – until they are converted into Thom's Megalithic Yards and the principles of Megalithic geometry applied. For all three of the solar system's main bodies (from a human perspective) to conform to such total accuracy proves the existence of the pattern.

How did the ancients come to possess such knowledge?

Finally, we must confront our greatest challenge: it is now time to attempt to make sense of all we have discovered. We must try to reconcile the existence of such miraculous knowledge with everything else that is known about the Neolithic peoples of western Europe and the early dynasties in Mesopotamia and Egypt.

No matter how hard we try, we find it impossible to believe that the Megalithic 366 system and its close 360 relative from Sumer were invented in isolation. There must surely be a connection – and a very direct connection at that. While it is entirely possible that both the Megalithic and Sumerian peoples could have estimated the circumference of the Earth using simple geometry and careful observation, we do not believe that they could have calculated the planet's mass or accurately assessed the dimensions of the Moon and the Sun.

The available archaeological evidence paints a picture of the Neolithic population of the British Isles as being very primitive, without a written language, metals or any kind of wheel. The pottery left by the Grooved Ware people is very crude and everything we know about these people points to short, hard lives. Despite these undeniable facts, this is the culture that built robust structures, durable enough to have survived more than 5,000 years. The existence of the Megalithic Yard at the sites surveyed by Thom confirms an ability to work to fine tolerances and indicates that the people concerned were aware of the concepts that we label pi and phi today.

But how did they arrive at the Megalithic Yard, that fascinating, and to many archaeologists, extremely frustrating unit of 0.8296656 metres?

We have described in detail how the individual builder could create a rule of a known length by following a relatively simple procedure and we have explained why this length was seen as so special in terms of the Earth's polar circumference. The Megalithic Yard can be accurately determined by any artisan with a knowledge of the prescribed technique of observing the turning Earth and swinging a pendulum. It takes no more than an average IQ to learn to reproduce a Megalithic Yard – but what can we deduce about the individuals who originated this unit that so beautifully fits the Earth, the Sun and the Moon?: that when applied to cubes, creates weights and capacities that are part of the modern imperial system. Surely, no Megalithic astronomer cum stonemason knew any of this?

Being as open-minded as it is possible to be, we cannot believe that the Megalithic builders could have defined the Megalithic Yard either by accident or design. And yet someone did.

Then there is the kush, the Sumerian/Babylonian unit that does not have any obvious connection to Earth's dimensions but which does define the second of time and produces astounding decimal/sexagesimal integers when used to describe the speed of light and the speed of the Earth's motion around the Sun. Again, we simply cannot believe that the Sumerians had any more 'true' understanding of the implications of the kush units than an African bushman has regarding the innermost workings of his clockwork radio. So, how did these ancient civilizations come to possess such knowledge?

Civilization One

For all the world it feels as though both Megalithic Man and the Sumerians shared the same teacher. The sudden development of brilliant cultures after more than 5,000 generations of humanity and the absence of any audit trail strongly suggests the intervention of a third party that is no longer known.

The principle of formal logic known as Occam's Razor states that 'entities are not to be multiplied without necessity'. This means that that elaborate solutions should not be created where simple ones will do. And we can think of no simpler solution than to accept that the contemporary records of the first civilizations actually mean exactly what they say!

Unfortunately there are no documentary records of Neolithic traditions – but we know that the Sumerians and Ancient Egyptians specifically stated that a group of people with, what appeared to them to be, god-like powers arrived from somewhere unknown to instruct them in the sciences and teach them skills in manufacturing. These 'Watchers' were thought of as gods, but it is said that they looked like normal people and they lived and died just like everyone else. While it is fashionable today to dismiss old myth and legend as little more than fairy stories, we believe that this explanation holds more water than any other.

Is this solution so preposterous that we have to overlook the obvious? Stepping back from the arrogance of the belief that our current civilization simply has to be the pinnacle of all human achievement leaves us wondering, 'Why on Earth do we have to accuse our forebears of writing down nonsense?'

The first response of any archaeologist to this thesis will be, 'So where is the archaeological evidence to support the notion of such a group of advanced people?' This is an entirely fair and reasonable question but our answer lies in information that we have brought forward from our forensic examination of measurement systems. The evidence outlined in this book appears to have demolished the standard idea that there was a slow, incremental improvement of humankind's understanding of science and nature from Stone Age to Internet Age.

Like Charles Dickens' Mr Gradgrind, we love facts, and we set out to find more facts than had previously been available. The whole idea of a 'Civilization One' is not going to appeal to many academics – and we fully understand why. This kind of notion has to be treated with great caution. Yet it does explain how these fantastically sophisticated units existed in cultures that were otherwise rather unsophisticated.

Could it be that there was once a single, highly-advanced group that virtually kick-started the world's first civilizations? If so, it appears that it failed in the case of the Megalithic culture because it seems to have died out. And yet in a way it never will, as long as any person on the planet orders a pound of apples or downs a pint of beer.

Others may identify a different solution, but in our estimation it would be impossible to create this interrelated Megalithic/Mesopotamian measurement matrix from a cold start. In other words, the Earth, Moon and Sun as well as the speed of light and the orbiting Earth would have to be measured using some arbitrary units before it would be possible to create units that produced such wonderful integer results. If we are correct regarding this point, the inference has to be that Civilization One was as advanced as the modern world, though far, far back in time during the period we refer to as prehistoric.

Another important point to consider is the way that the numbers we have found work. Everything about the Megalithic system hinges on the value of 366 and the Sumerian/Babylonian system works on their sexagesimal principle. But there are many instances where the integers fall out in decimal terms:

1,000 Minoan feet to an Earth Second of arc

100 Megalithic Yards to a lunar second of arc

40,000 Megalithic Yards to a solar second of arc

We are well aware that some people will say that we have found meaning because we have seen big round numbers in base 10. They might argue that despite the bizarre 'coincidence' of all three solar system objects producing these results when using ancient measures, all numbers are equally valid and that they would not look anything special if we used another base. The number 100, for example, would read as 144 in base 8. This point is valid – but our whole argument is that some human beings in the very distant past realized that the Earth was precisely 3.66 times larger than the Moon and that the Sun was 400 times larger. Having 10 digits on their hands they had naturally worked in base 10 and saw the relationship as follows:

Moon – 100

Earth – 366

Sun – 40,000

Having observed and understood this remarkable relationship these people also recognized that the value 366 was important to the Earth because that was the number of rotations it had on its axis in the course of one solar orbit. And a 366th part of the day was the difference between the solar and sidereal day. Furthermore, there was a reciprocal relationship because the Earth had 10,000 days to 366 lunar days. Having digested these facts it is little wonder that these early astronomers considered the Earth to be a 366 phenomenon and then proceeded to work out a unit of measure that unified this knowledge.

But these people, whoever they were, also understood the mass of the Earth in great detail and realized that the '366ness' of our planet goes even deeper. They used a pendulum to beat 366 times during Venus' movement across a 366th part of the horizon, and produced a pendulum length that corresponded precisely to the units that describe the circumferences of the Earth, Moon and Sun. This surely verges on the magical.

Everything here must be the result of some very smart calculations by the surveyors from Civilization One. Equally, the Sumerian decimal/ sexagesimal results for the speed of light and the orbiting Earth could have been carefully and deliberately calculated. Nevertheless, no matter how bright the theoretical scientists of Civilization One might have been, there are some issues arising here that transcend any human power.

The speed of light is believed to be a fixed phenomenon and anyone clever enough can certainly use it to define multiple integer length against time. But no-one can have influenced the speed of the Earth's orbit around the Sun – it is what it is. So, the following has to be a coincidence:

Earth's orbital speed = one 10,000th of the speed of light

Furthermore, using NASA data, we found that the diameter of our planet's motion around the Sun is almost exactly 600×10^6 kush per Sumerian second. This is a perfect Sumerian sexagesimal number yet again and it means that light travels across the disc of the Earth's orbit in a strangely neat 1,000 seconds.

Factors like these must be coincidences – they are all such human numbers, as though the very 'blueprint' of our solar system was saying, 'Recognize that all this has been designed for you 10-fingered humans.'

Under any normal circumstances these kinds of fit would not be dismissed as a coincidence. But here the conclusion may be too unsettling for many because, if they are not random, then maybe our work does not really concern archaeologists at all. Add these observations to the other well-known improbability of the Moon's very existence and perhaps we should be speaking to a scientifically-minded theologian! The consequences of these truths have certainly shaken our previously rather agnostic worldview.

We have discounted the idea that the Neolithic inhabitants of western Europe could have created the so-called Megalithic system or that the Sumerians could have devised the kush/second system. It has been necessary to assume that a highly-developed civilization must have existed in prehistory – just as the world's oldest history books state. But how clever is it possible for any human to be?

We have agonized over this for many months. We are not religious people and we know that to invoke a deity is normally a lazy 'cop out' – a way of ignoring a problem by sticking a 'God' label on anything we cannot explain. While neither of us would ever have denied the possible existence of a creative force that permeates the universe, turning chaos into order, we would never previously have seen any basis for anything approaching a deliberate plan. Now we are a great deal less sure. Maybe everything we have found can be explained in terms of physics – but that would not change anything. Freemasons use the term 'Great Architect of the Universe' and 'Grand Geometrician of the Universe' so that people of all religions can come together without having to fall out about the mythical name. These masonic designations appear to be particularly appropriate.

We have resisted the idea for as long as we can but we have had to concede that it does look as though our place in universe has been designed, and that the designer has laid down some very deliberate clues so that we will recognize the plan. Such thoughts amount to a form of 'blasphemy' to the atheist, whose worldview requires absolute, cold rationality. But what happens to the ultra-pragmatist when the evidence suddenly points the other way?

Consider this: if the 'Great Architect of the Universe' had a special place for mankind – as most world religions believe – and that Architect wanted to reveal their actions to a 10-fingered creature, they would surely communicate in base 10. That would be a way of saying, 'Pay attention – I'm talking to you'.

When the chosen species had developed sufficiently it would begin to understand its environment and measure it using units derived from the Architect's chosen order and counted in base 10.

These 'chosen ones' would realize that the message was timed, because the Moon has not always been one four-hundredth of the distance between the Earth and the Sun, although it has always been one four-hundredth the size of the Sun. It would dawn on them that the Earth orbits the Sun at one-tenth the speed of light and that the circle of the orbit takes 100 seconds for light to traverse it.

We can hear the grinding of scientific teeth as we dare to print these observations and that is excusable, if not reasonable. But we are equally sure that some who hold firm religious convictions will be outraged by these notions. They will still want to believe in the ancient myths, but for them the Creator's direct involvement in human matters only happened in some distant past when Moses, Gautama Buddha, Zoroaster, Jesus Christ or Muhammad walked the Earth.

It seems to us that there must have been a Civilization One; an advanced people who trained the rest of the world in science and technology, thereby leading it out of the Stone Age. But surely these forgotten people understood the message that was calling to them from the very fabric of nature. The people that are spoken of in ancient records taught the world about God and the great plan of nature. But the message became jumbled and almost lost as modern humankind began to believe in its own importance as the pinnacle of all intellectual achievement. Perhaps fortunately, the essence of the message has never been totally lost. By some mechanism, units such as the pound and the pint live on, and the giant stones of the Megalithic builders stood sufficiently upright to be read by at least one engineer with the genius to unravel their hidden secret. There is infinitely more to all this than we have touched upon as yet.

So far, we have not discovered how or why Megalithic units of length should define weights and measures that match imperial units such as the pound and the pint. We are particularly interested in the families and institutions involved in the emergence of these medieval French units and we have a great deal more research to conduct, though there are tantalizing clues that offer a whole new line of enquiry for the future.

We believe that this closing chapter of our first investigative book together is the beginning of our next great challenge. The real work begins now.

Earth Days and Proving the Megalithic Yard

The Earth spins on its axis (relative to any star) just over 366 times in one orbit of the Sun, one sidereal year, as against the solar year, which is shorter. Therefore, each rotation of the Earth also represents one degree of the great circle of the heavens that is the planet's solar orbit. From an earthbound perspective it appears that the Sun moves just under one degree along the plane of the ecliptic each day.

Most people understand that there are 365.2564 days in a year, but many do not appreciate there are 366.2564 turns of the Earth on its own axis during the same period. This apparent contradiction comes about because a full rotation of the Earth does not take the same period of time as that between one sunrise and the next. Most of the angular movement of the Sun that we see as it passes across the sky is indeed caused by the spinning of the Earth on its axis but a small part is caused by the Earth's orbit about the Sun. If the Earth was turning on its axis but not revolving about the Sun, the Sun would appear to remain in a fixed place relative to the background stars and a day on Earth would be exactly the same as one spin of the planet.

Conversely, if the Earth was not revolving on its axis, but simply travelling round the Sun, while facing the same direction in space, the Sun would then appear to go round the sky exactly once a year – and

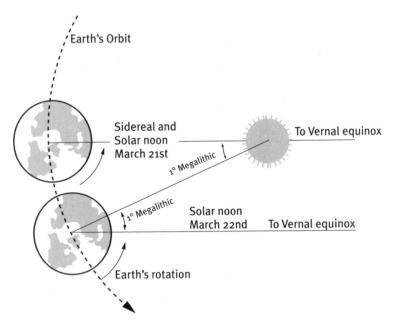

The earth turns once on its axis for each Megalithic degree of solar orbit.

we would have one day per year. As this apparent movement goes in the opposite direction to the spin of the Earth it takes exactly one day off the 'real' year of $366^1/_4$ spins of our planet giving us the familiar $365^1/_4$-day year.

In summary, according to our earthbound view of the Sun, there appear to be just over 365 solar days of 86,400 seconds but, according to the stars, there are just over 366 sidereal days of 86,164 seconds each. It follows that a 366-degree circle is a very logical invention for an early culture that is interested in astronomy, as the Neolithic people of western Europe are known to have been.

The Method for Establishing the Megalithic Yard

When viewed from Earth, the movements of the Venus within the zodiac are extremely complex yet, with an appropriate technique, an

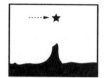

Night 1
A star aligns with a fixed
point before moving west

Night 2
The same star appears
from the east

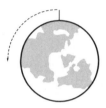

The Earth has revolved once on its axis and travelled through
one Megalithic degree of its solar orbit

One turn of the Earth can be gauged by marking the position of a star.

accurate unit of linear measurement can be achieved by appropriate observation of this planet's movements.

Venus, after passing across the face of the Sun (known as the inferior conjunction or transit) rises ahead of it by anything up to two hours or more, and precedes it across the sky. So bright is Venus (known in this form as 'the morning star') in the reflected light of the Sun that it can be seen during the lightest part of the day if one knows where to look. Eventually, after approximately 72 days, it reaches its maximum elongation as the morning star (the greatest apparent distance from the Sun when viewed from Earth). It then drops back towards the Sun and crosses in a superior conjunction, after which it emerges as what is known as 'the evening star'. In a repeat of its daytime movement it gradually moves away from the Sun, eventually setting after it. Ultimately, it reaches maximum elongation and then falls back towards to the Sun to begin its cycle again.

During these movements (which are directly related to the fact that the Earth is also travelling around the Sun) Venus takes a peculiar path through the zodiac. For periods of about two weeks at a time (and sometimes more), Venus moves quickly through the zodiac, bettering the Sun's 59 minutes of arc per day by up to 17 minutes of arc. At other times, because the Earth is catching up to Venus as it too travels around the Sun, Venus can appear to stand still or even fall back within the zodiac. At such times it is referred to as being 'retrograde'.

It is during its most rapid movement within the zodiac that Venus presents itself as the perfect 'clock' against which to check the half Megalithic Yard pendulum. At these times a Venus day can exceed the sidereal day by 303 seconds of time. (This Venus day being an Earth day that can be measured between Venus appearing at a specific point relative to a point on the horizon and it doing so again the next day.) This makes such a Venus day 86,467 seconds in length, as opposed to 186,164 seconds for the sidereal day.

When using Venus passing between the suggested angled framework in order to check the pendulum across one 366th of the horizon or sky, it will be observed that this planet behaves slightly differently to a star. Because Venus is also travelling in the opposite direction to the turning sky, it will take longer to pass across the one Megalithic-degree gap than would a star. Let us look at an example set for Orkney, Scotland, where we estimate such calculations must have regularly been made by our Megalithic ancestors.

One Venus day (with the planet travelling at maximum speed within the zodiac) is equal to 86,467 seconds

This means that in order to complete 1 Megalithic Degree, Venus would take 236.2486388 seconds. One 366th of this figure is 0.64548807071 seconds and this should be the period of one beat of the half Megalithic Yard pendulum if Venus was to reliably do the job we expect of it.

Meanwhile, we need to discover the time taken for one beat of a half Megalithic Yard pendulum of 41.48328 centimetres at Orkney. The acceleration due to gravity at this latitude is 981.924 centimetres/second^2. A quick calculation tells us that one beat of such a pendulum would take 0.64572263956 seconds.

The difference between the theoretical timing for a Venus pendulum and the true half Megalithic Yard pendulum in this case is 0.00023456885 seconds, which equates to a difference in the size of the full Megalithic Yard of 0.05 millimetres. Alexander Thom found that the Megalithic Yard was 82.96656 centimetres to within a tolerance of + or − 0.06 millimetres. Therefore Venus proves to be an ideal pendulum-setting clock in this case.

We are suggesting that the Megalithic Yard could be checked and set at any latitude between 60 degrees north at the uppermost extreme, down to around 48 degrees north in its southern ranges. Although acceleration due to gravity alters slightly at differing latitudes, we found that the Venus-derived half and therefore full Megalithic Yard defined at any latitude from Orkney down to Brittany remained within Professor Thom's findings.

It would be incredible to believe that the involvement of Venus, being so perfectly tuned to this experiment, is nothing more than a peculiar coincidence – particularly since the ability of the planet to act as a clock only occurs when it is travelling as fast as it is capable of doing within the zodiac. It is not possible to obtain a Megalithic Yard by this method that is 'longer' than that found by Alexander Thom. It could therefore be suggested that if our Megalithic ancestors had carried out their experiment during every day across the whole of a Venus cycle, the 'longest' half Megalithic Yard pendulum they could achieve would be the correct one. In reality this would not have been necessary because we are certain they knew exactly when to take their readings (see Appendix 5).

Remarkable as these findings are, the truly amazing fact is that those using the method managed to remain so incredibly accurate, since the deviations found by Professor Thom are so very small. This is indeed a tribute to our Megalithic ancestors who were not only great naked-eye astronomers but also very careful engineers.

The full procedure is itemized below.

1. Create a pendulum by taking a round pebble and make a hole in the centre to pass a piece of twine through (used as a plumb bob to find verticals by Megalithic builders).
2. Draw a large circle on the ground, in an area with a good view of the horizon and sky. Divide the perimeter of the circle into 366 equal parts. This is quite simply done by trial and error but it is almost certain that the Megalithic astronomers knew that a circle with a diameter of 233 units would have a circumference of 732 of the same units (732 being twice 366). They could therefore arrange a diameter of 233 units (any units will do) and then mark off two units on the circumference to identify one 366th of the horizon.
3. Build a braced framework across one 366th division of the circumference of the circle, which can be angled so that it is at 90 degrees to the angle of the path of the rising (or setting)

Venus at that latitude.

4. Observe the framework from the centre of the circle. When Venus passes into the braced framework, begin swinging the pendulum. Some initial trial and error is called for, but when exactly 366 beats of the pendulum take place while Venus is traversing the $1/366$ gap, the pendulum must be a half Megalithic Yard in length.

5. Repeat the experiment on successive nights if necessary, to account for the differing speed of Venus within the zodiac. The longest pendulum achieved during the full cycle of Venus will be exactly half of the most accurate geodetic Megalithic Yard.

Note: This technique represents one way in which the Megalithic builders could have reproduced the half Megalithic Yard. Time and study might provide others. This horizon method could be subject to very slight inaccuracy as a result of 'refraction' of the rising or setting Venus when it is close to the horizon. (Refraction is the distortion of the size or position of an object caused by atmospheric conditions and proximity to the horizon.) It is most likely that Venus was tracked when it was above approximately 15 degrees above the horizon, in order to obviate distortion due to refraction.

Our astronomical associate, Peter Harwood, considers that on balance the setting Venus may have been used, rather than Venus rising as a morning star, though his consideration here has more to do with ease of observation than as a result of any technical considerations.

The Formula for Finding the Volume of a Sphere

In Chapter 3 we discussed the capacity of cubes with sides of a length that conform to the Megalithic system, for example the 4 Megalithic-Inch cube that would hold one imperial pint of water. But we also experimented with spheres, both of the same and of different Megalithic sizes as the cubes.

In order for interested readers to be able to check our findings for themselves, we thought it might be useful for those whose schooldays may be now far behind them to be reminded of how the volume of a sphere is achieved.

The formula is as follows: $^4/_3 \pi r^3$. So, for example, if we want to establish the volume of a sphere of 5 Megalithic Inches in diameter (10.37082 centimetres) we first need to establish the radius, which in this case is 5.18541 centimetres.

The radius cubed is 139.4277 cubic centimetres.

Multiplying this by π we arrive at 438.0252 and $^4/_3$ of this is 584 cubic centimetres.

In the case of a 6 Megalithic-Inch diameter sphere (12.444984 centimetres) the radius will be 6.222492 centimetres.

The radius cubed will be 240.931198 cubic centimetres.

Multiplying this by π we arrive at 756.9076 and $^4/_3$ of this is 1,009 cubic centimetres.

More about Megalithic Music

Music appears to be not only interesting but also absolutely essential to our species. Our research could not turn up one culture, contemporary or historical, that has been shown to be without music and rhythm. Indeed, experiments carried out in prehistoric caves and the structures created by our Megalithic ancestors seem to indicate that even the acoustic capabilities of natural and created structures have been important to humanity for many thousands of years.[1] Archaeologists have also discovered percussive instruments and extremely well-made bone and antler flutes of Stone Age date.

Developing civilizations have classified music in a number of different ways. In the modern western method of musical notation there are considered to be eight notes to a scale of music, allowing for the fact that the starting note and finishing note are the same, but one octave apart, for example C, D, E, F, G, A, B and C again.

The tuning of musical instruments has long been a problem. If the method of tuning by fifths (supposedly credited to Pythagoras) is employed, it is not possible to play a particular instrument in different keys without retuning it because some notes will sound discordant. In order to compensate for this difficulty, western culture has adopted a

---

[1] Devereux, P.: *Stone Age Soundtracks*. Vega, London, 2001.

228

method known as 'even tempered tuning', which allows a compensation to be 'written into' the tuning that spreads the accumulating pitch problem in such a way that most ears cannot identify the discrepancies.

The modern convention of having eight notes to an octave is by no means the only possibility. Across the world there have been and still are many other ways of handling the musical scale and none is more correct than any other. It follows therefore that the pitch of specific notes will also vary from culture to culture.

The tuning of musical instruments was once a very local matter. All that concerned the musicians was that their instruments were in tune, one with another. But as soon as music began to cross boundaries, local tunings were no longer possible, especially for many woodwind and brass instruments that are not easily retuned. As a result, much of the world now conforms to international concert tuning, in which each note has a specific frequency, for example A, which is 440 Hz.

It was because of international concert tuning that we were able to define Megalithic mathematics and geometry in musical terms. As the Earth turns on its axis the 366 degrees of the Megalithic divisions of the Earth at the equator pass across a given point in one sidereal day. If we look at the situation in terms of the Megalithic Yard, we know that one Megalithic Second of arc of the Earth has a linear distance of 366 Megalithic Yards. Using Megalithic geometry it is possible to work out the frequencies involved.

A Megalithic Second is more than a geometric division as far as the Earth is concerned. It is also a finite measurement of time and is equal to 0.653946 modern seconds of time. This is how long it takes the Earth to turn one Megalithic Second of arc on its axis. We have called one beat per Megalithic Second of time one Thom, or Th, and since there are 366 Megalithic Yards to a Megalithic Second of arc of the Earth, there are 366 Megalithic Yard beats to one Megalithic Second of time (one 366 Th). If we translate this into modern musical conventions and modern timekeeping, 366 Th is equal to 560 Hz, which in international concert tuning would give a note a little above C# (C sharp). But this is looking at things in terms of frequency. If we think about the Megalithic Yard in terms of wavelength, we discover that 82.96656 centimetres produces a wavelength very close to that relating to the note we would presently call G#, so both C# and G# could be said to have a very special relationship with the Megalithic system.

With regard to rhythm, 1 beat per Megalithic second is the same as a modern expression of timing of 91.5 beats per minute. Using simple harmonics, timings of 15.25, 30.5, 45.75, 61, 76.25, 106.75, 122, 137.25, 152.5, 177.5 and also 183 beats per minute would seem to be appropriate, in the sense that they all have a harmonic relationship with 91.5 beats per minute. We therefore looked at as much indigenous music as we could from around the world in order to establish whether or not Megalithic music actually existed and in order to understand if there might be something instinctive about these pitches and timings. As far as was possible we restricted ourselves to pieces of music with a rhythms shown above and to pieces played in either C# or G#.

It would certainly not be fair to suggest that anything like all indigenous music conforms to these patterns, because it definitely does not. Neither do we claim that we have carried out a valid scientific experiment in the case. What we can report is that we came across music from many different parts of the world that conformed in whole or part to the Megalithic system, and that these pitches and timings appear to show up more regularly than chance would dictate.

Both the key and the rhythm were common among indigenous North American cultures, where many of the sampled chants and songs are particularly significant with regard to their rhythmic patterns. We found some examples in South America, though much of that music has been affected by Spanish and other influences and authentic recordings of Pre-Columbian music are hard to come by.

Examples of old long-playing records created on site in Senegal, Ethiopia, Morocco and Algeria proved interesting and appeared to demonstrate strong elements of the patterns we were seeking in Africa. Some of the best examples came from much further north and east however, with Tibetan Buddhist chants showing a strong resemblance to Megalithic rhythms and keys. Probably related were Siberian songs, particularly those created by 'overtone' or 'throat' singers, some of which proved to be near perfect examples of Megalithic tunings and rhythms. Australian Aboriginal songs were also interesting, the more so because C# didgeridoos are extremely common. Rhythms vary markedly between examples we have collected, but 91.5 beats per minute, together with its mathematical subdivisions and multiples, are not uncommon.

The greatest difficulty in this research lies in the fact that even ethnic songs and tunes are now invariably recorded in studios, where the natural inclinations of musicians, both in terms of rhythm and tuning, are subservient to the requirements of modern recording techniques. This could also account for the fact that in places such as the British Isles, it is almost impossible to access true, indigenous music. Many English, Scottish, Welsh and Irish traditional songs approximate Megalithic rhythms, but it is impossible to say for certain that this is the case. Timings of 100 beats per minute are extremely common but we suspect this owes more to engineers using electronic metres rather than to the natural caprices of musicians or the turning of our planet.

APPENDIX 4

Music and Light

In all our discoveries during the research for this book the potential association between sound, specifically music, and light has proved to be one of the most surprising. We fully appreciate that science does not recognize a relationship between these two apparently unrelated phenomena and we have itemized the generally-stated differences between them below.

Sound is created by a source, for example a clanging bell, and sound waves represent generally small areas of high and low pressure caused by the sound source. These variations in pressure cannot travel except through a medium, so in outer space nobody can hear you scream. However, sound can travel through wood, metal, paper, plastic, water, sulphuric acid or almost any other medium. Much of the time sound travels to our ears via the atmosphere.

Sound can be thought of as similar to waves in water, which pass outward, like ripples caused on a pond when a stone is thrown into the water. The ear of any animal, including a human being, is specifically designed to detect the differences in pressure caused by sound waves and to pass these on to the brain, where they are interpreted as sounds. Like all waves, sound waves have frequency, so they can be measured in hertz (cycles per second).

Light waves form part of the electromagnetic spectrum. All electromagnetic waves emanate from bodies such as suns. They are caused by charged particles thrown off from such bodies, which can travel across great distances to reach us here on the Earth. Electromagnetic waves cover a large number of frequencies from very high-frequency shortwave gamma rays, up to extremely low-frequency longwave radio waves. Many parts of the electromagnetic spectrum are harnessed by humanity, for example radio, television, electrical power, X-rays, microwaves and so on. The very world we inhabit only gave birth to life because of the electromagnetic spectrum. Plants cannot live without light, which they transpose into energy, and if it were not for plant life we could not exist either.

Visible light is only one form of radiation that forms a tiny part (about 1,000th) of the electromagnetic spectrum; other creatures can see parts of the visible spectrum that humans cannot. Typically, humans can see light with frequencies between 4×10^{14} Hz to 8.1×10^{14} Hz. When split by a prism into its component parts, light provides a multitude of colours, varying from red at one end of the spectrum to violet at the other. In common usage these colours are often referred to as red, orange, yellow, green, blue, indigo and violet but in reality there is no line of demarcation between any two colours. The computer on which the typescript of this book was written is capable of producing many millions of different colours.

The reason we see colours is that parts of the visible spectrum are absorbed by things – both animate and inanimate – upon which they fall, while others are reflected. The light that falls into our eyes represents the reflected frequencies. So, for example, since most plants do not absorb green light, it is reflected back into our eyes. The radiation from these reflections falls onto receptors in our eyes, which pass the information to our brains, where it is interpreted as colour.

The only real relationship between sound waves and light waves is that they possess frequency and wavelength, which is why they are measured in the same way. However, as we demonstrated in Chapter 11, the relationship may exist at a physiological level, rather than as a fact of physics. Our suggestion is that any biological entity, for example ourselves, that develops a sense such as hearing, which operates across a given range of frequencies, may develop other senses, such as sight, across frequencies that have a resonant relationship with the sound waves.

Resonance is simply explained by a person walking into a room while carrying a tuning fork, set to vibrate at, say, 440 Hz. If the tuning fork is struck and the room contains a multitude of other silent tuning forks, some of these are likely to begin vibrating, apparently of their own accord. Let us suppose that there were tuning forks in the room set to vibrate as 220 Hz and 880 Hz. Each of these bears a frequency relationship to the 440 Hz fork. Musically speaking, the 440 Hz tuning fork would create the sound we know as the A below middle C on a piano; 220 Hz is also the note A, but an octave lower, and 880 Hz is A again, though this time one octave higher. This doubling or halving of frequency, at least in Western music, is called 'an octave'. The tuning fork we struck set up a 'sympathetic resonance' with other tuning forks in the room, which is why they too began to sing.

There are two significant factors regarding visible light that seem to ally it at some level with sound, and specifically music. First, the part of the electromagnetic spectrum covered by visible light runs from about 4×10^{14} Hz to 8.1×10^{14} Hz. This represents a doubling of frequency, so in musical terms it can be called an octave. The second association occurs when one considers the difference in frequency between musical notes and the frequency of visible light. The note we have designated as Megalithic C, which is 558 Hz, when doubled 40 times, brings us to a frequency within the visible part of the electromagnetic spectrum.

Forty doublings or octaves up in terms of frequency, 558 Hz becomes 6.13527×10^{14} Hz, which represents the colour blue and appears right in the middle of the human visual spectrum in terms of frequency.

There may be no tangible connection between the musical note of Megalithic C and the colour blue that can be tied down by physics, but it is possible that within the brain sound and light are dealt with in a similar manner. It may therefore be no coincidence that we have evolved to see in colours that have frequencies that maintain a resonant relationship with the sounds we hear.

APPENDIX 5

The Phaistos Disc and the Megalithic Year

In Chapter 2 we explained the method by which we believe our Megalithic ancestors replicated the half Megalithic Yard pendulum, in order to validate the geodetic Megalithic Yard, which they had already established.

All the available evidence points to the fact that rather than using a star and a pendulum, as we had first considered, the astronomer-priests of the Megalithic Period had used a pendulum and the planet Venus. However, such a technique relies on a certain knowledge of which 'days' during the complex movements of the planet Venus are appropriate for the procedure.

It might occur to some readers, as it did to us, that the smallest irregularity in the calendar could lead to great mistakes in such a system when establishing the correct days to use in any Venus cycle, because unregistered drift of the cycles of Venus across time could lead to the wrong result. Within the very small tolerances he observes, Alexander Thom showed that the Megalithic Yard remained remarkably consistent, probably across as much as 2,000 years. In our estimation the Megalithic builders had two answers to this problem, the first being the knowledge that the longest half Megalithic Yard pendulum achieved from the Venus observations was the one they were looking for. However, of just as much importance would be a very good understanding of the 'real' year, together with some knowledge of the Venus cycles themselves.

The way the Venus cycle meshes with that of the Earth was of great significance to these early calendar creators. They would certainly have noticed that for every five 'apparent' full cycles of Venus, eight Earth years pass. However, this could only be fully appreciated if the actual length of the earth year was understood. Even using the modern calendar, this can be somewhat misleading .

We presently use a fairly hotchpotch system of corrections that have gradually evolved since Roman times. Our first course of action is to add an extra day to the civil calendar every four years – which then becomes known as a leap year. However, this procedure is not accurate enough and because it over-compensates, we don't add a leap year in century years – unless they are millennium years. Although this system is fine for routine purposes and sorts itself out over a long period of time, it is capable of being quite wrong at any given point, certainly by more than a day.

Such a state of affairs could have caused real complications to a culture that simply had to keep a tight rein on the true year and this fact alone tends to suggest that our Megalithic ancestors had built themselves a very accurate calendar. In fact there is evidence that this was the case.

Our hypothesis suggests that the Megalithic civil year was 366 days in length, which in terms of the real year would appear to be even further adrift than our year of 365 days, but what really matters is the compensation techniques that were made to bring the civil year and the true year together.

Alan's time spent studying the Phaistos Disc strongly suggested that

The Phaistos Disc, side A.

it had been designed for a year of 366 days. The Phaistos Disc was created by the civilization on Crete that we now know as the Minoan culture, and was manufactured about 2000 BC. It was found in the ruins of the Minoan palace of Phaistos, in the south of Crete, and it is now kept in the nearby Heraklion Museum.

The Disc is made of fired clay. Prior to firing, each its sides was given incised spiral lines, inside of which stand groups of hieroglyphic characters pressed into the clay using stamps or dies. The two sides of the Phaistos Disc are shown above.

238

The Phaistos Disc, side B.

Linguists and other interested parties have for years tried to translate the message of the Phaistos Disc and despite some valiant efforts, the general opinion is that all of them have failed. The reason is quite simple. We have no knowledge of the language spoken in Minoan Crete and without that, or some sort of Minoan 'Rosetta Stone', interpretation of the characters would seem to be impossible.

It was not so much what the characters might say that interested Alan, however, but rather the number of them on each side of the Disc, and how those numbers might relate to each other. The first fact of note is that the characters fall within spirals. Many researchers now think that there are occasions when spirals are meant to indicate the passing of the Sun throughout the year, as is suggested to be the case of the spirals carved at Newgrange in Ireland's Boyne Valley. This was the first clue that the Phaistos Disc might be some sort of calendar.

It took several years of research and a whole book to explain what Alan discovered, partly because the Phaistos Disc is, in fact, a multi-faceted aid to calculation, though there is one particular job it does quite brilliantly. Side A of the Disc contains 123 hieroglyphs, and side B has 119. If these are viewed as simple markers, irrespective of what they might say, then the Disc can be shown to comprise a 'second calendar' specifically manufactured to run alongside the 366-day calendar and to identify the times when compensations need to be made in order to reconcile the 366-day year and the true year.

The procedure for using the Disc as described above is very simple. Every symbol on side A is counted, most likely from the centre out and one for each day, until the end of the spiral is reached. All of these symbols, 123 in total, relate to the centre symbol in side B of the Disc. Now all the symbols on side A are counted again, this time relating to the second symbol on side B. The procedure is repeated time and again until 123 days has elapsed for each of the 119 symbols on side B. The total number of days indicated by the Disc is 14,637. This is extremely close to 40 years of 366 days, which would total 14,640 days. Probably the Disc is perpetual, and so simply continues a new series of cycles, but as if to premeditate this important 40-year period, those creating the Disc added three dots at the end of the spiral to indicate the missing three days necessary to make the full 40-year cycle of 14,640 days. (The dots were present to 'demonstrate' the full 40-year cycle but were not used in the calendar round explained below.)

The ingenuity of this system is that it told those using the Disc when it was necessary to compensate for the inaccuracies that were accruing between the ritual year and real year. The vital period is 4 x 123 days (492 days), at which time one day would be literally removed from the ritual 366-day calendar. It would be as if that day never existed. For example, and in our terms, the calendar might jump from 1st March to 3rd March.

We can find no better method of compensating for a 366-day year than to remove 1 day every 492 days. Such a procedure would keep the civil calendar and the real calendar in harmony for well over 3,000 years without any other alteration being necessary. This is a phenomenal feat and any observer would be forced to admit that it is neater and more accurate than the system we use today.

The Phaistos Disc is capable of much more than this little miracle and it almost certainly has additional capabilities that we have not yet recognized. Everything known about it so far is itemized in *The Bronze Age Computer Disc*. However, it was the existence of the 123-day, or more properly in this context, the 492-day alternative calendar that alerted Alan to the presence in Crete of the 366-day year he had already suspected must have once existed.

It is not possible for this method of compensation to ever see the civil year and the true year at odds by more than 0.75 of a day, and even this inaccuracy can only exist for a maximum of 126 days. The larger discrepancies of our own calendar simply do not occur in this system.

Another feature of the Phaistos Disc is that it supplies an extremely accurate calendar for the behaviour and movements of the planets Mercury and Venus. If the hieroglyphics are replaced with modern numerals, what we get is an extremely accurate planetary ready-reckoner. So obvious was this that Alan soon came to appreciate that there was a simple rule of thumb, particularly for the planet Venus, that he had not recognized before. When using 366-day years the rule is this: any phenomena of Venus that takes place today will happen again 40 years less 40 days from now. For those conversant with the procedures itemized by the Disc, it would have been child's play to catalogue and remember those times when Venus could be used to achieve an accurate Megalithic Yard. Although the procedure is straight-forward, the explanation of it is not, and since this book is not directly connected to the Phaistos Disc research, we refer interested readers who wish to know more to *The Bronze Age Computer Disc*.

APPENDIX 6

The Amazing Barley Seed

Modern understanding of Sumerian and Old Babylonian measuring systems has been reconstructed by experts who have studied many cuneiform texts found on clay tablets in the ruins of ancient cities of Mesopotamia. Like many long-lived cultures, the various linear lengths, weights and volumes used in the 'Fertile Crescent' can be terribly complicated, with specific lengths or weights often reserved for a particular commodity. However, as we suggested in Chapter 4, there are certain weights and measures that were used as standards, and which did not change significantly over time. According to Professor Livio C. Stecchini these units stem from the Sumerian Period, circa 1800 BC.

The smallest unit of length associated with the Sumerians and the Babylonians was the 'se' which meant 'barley seed'. There were 6 se to one shu-si and 360 se to the double-kush. Most experts in Mesopotamian metrology would not argue with these figures and it seemed reasonable to us that the se or barley seed, being the smallest denomination of length, weight and volume, should offer the perfect starting point for understanding the entire system. We had been somewhat surprised when an expert in this area of research answered our request for more information about the barley seed as a Sumerian unit of measure by email in the following way:

'The barleycorns are more for calculational convenience rather than being considered as actual barleycorns.' [1]

Our response was to keep an open mind as to whether or not these ancient scientists actually meant what they said or whether it was indeed a kind of nickname for something small.

The standard 'calculational convenience' theory is quite understandable because in the British and many European measuring systems, the 'grain' existed as a term until the introduction of the metric system. In Britain, the grain was originally a true barley grain, though for some purposes wheat seeds were used. In the British and many of the western European systems, the grain eventually became a standard unit, often differing greatly from the humble seed that had been its origin.

Another reason why many archaeologists deny that the Sumerians were referring to real barley seed relates to information dealt with while we were working with the Sumerian cube, in Chapter 4. The supposed problem lies in the fact that 180 x 60 is the number of barley seeds in both a mana (weight) and a sila (volume). Using the barley seed as a unit of weight, this could never be the case, since a mana is about 500 grams and a sila is about a litre, which, we are told, weighed almost exactly a kilogram. All the same, we felt obliged to look more closely at this Mesopotamian se or barley seed. We knew from the texts that a kush (cubit) was said to have a value of 180 barley seeds. When we tried the experiment for ourselves, it became immediately obvious why experts in the past had dismissed the barley seed as a reality in the system. Given that the kush was around half a metre, each barley seed would have to measure 2.77 millimetres. Our own experiments showed that the length of a modern barley seed, when laid end to end, averages

---

1 We have deliberately chosen not to name the professor in question. He was very helpful to our research and it is not our intention to embarrass him.

out at 8.46 millimetres. We might have left the situation at that, except for the fact that we decided to measure all the barley seed's dimensions.

If the seeds had been pierced in their centres and placed onto a very fine thread, as in a necklace, the seeds would have been on their sides. We did not thread the seeds but laid them out in a row on double-sided sticky tape (*see Colour Plate section*). When we did so, we discovered that they conformed incredibly well to the Sumerian/Babylonian model and there were indeed close to 180 barley seeds on average to the kush!

Taking the kush at 49.94 centimetres in length, each barley seed should measure 2.77 millimetres. The average width of our own sample of modern barley grains (using both large and small seeds at random and across a number of examples) was around 2.81mm, typically giving more than 177 to the kush. This is incredibly close to the hypothetical Sumerian model and tended to suggest that, at least in terms of physical dimensions, our own barley seeds were not greatly different to the Sumerian examples.

At this point the theory that 'barley seed' was merely a word used for 'calculational convenience' by the Sumerians was already looking less likely. As we thought about the Sumerians and Babylonians dividing the horizon (like all circles) into 360 degrees we realized that if the seeds were arranged in a curve to form a circle it would hold just a few more seeds. It turned out that a circle of 360 barley seems was indeed a double-kush in length – so each grain was precisely equal to one degree in this circle. Here was another example of Sumerian thinking, with circles within circles dancing to the number pattern based on 360.

We next turned our attention to the weight of the seeds. In order to obtain the 'intended' weight of the basic unit known as the mana, we performed the calculation outlined in Chapter 4, taking one-fifth the length of the kush and cubing it. The kush is 49.94 centimetres, a fifth of which is 9.988 centimetres. The cube of this is 996.404 cubic centimetres. The metric system says that the weight of water in such a cube would be 996.4 grams.

According to the cuneiform texts (or at least to the standard interpretation of them) there ought to be a total of 180 x 60 = 10,800 barley seeds in a mana. We already knew that the weight of a mana must be exactly half that of the sila and it is the sila that is created from the one-fifth kush cube. Put simply, this means that the mana is only half the value of the one-fifth kush cube and so should be expected to return a weight of 498.2 grams. If this weight is made up of 180 x 60 = 10,800 barley seeds, then each seed must weigh 46 milligrams.

We next measured the weight of our own barley seeds on a set of simple but accurate balance scales. In one pan, we placed a one gram weight, and in the other we began to place seeds, both large and small, until the scales balanced exactly. We repeated the procedure many times until we had a good average for the number of barley seeds necessary to balance the one-gram weight. The result was 21.5 seeds, meaning that our barley seeds weighed an average of 46.5 milligrams. For thoroughness we also checked this against independent figures, taken from the 1979 English crop, which averaged 45 milligrams per barley seed. Both our figures and those from the 1979 crop were so close to the expected Sumerian/Babylonian system that we were amazed how little our barley differed from that harvested more than 4,000 years ago. As a result of these findings, we are now confident about reconstructing the intended Sumerian measuring systems.

Judging by our own experiments, the originators of this system used a combination of large seeds from the centre of the ear of barley, and smaller ones from the ends of the ear. To obtain the definitive weight of one barley seed would have been impossible for the

Sumerians. The whole system is built around significant numbers of seeds, the better to gain an accurate average.

The beauty of the system lies in its simplicity. The linear length (kush) was originally derived from a pendulum with a period of one Sumerian second but the same unit could be reasonably accurately established by any buyer or seller in the marketplace by simply stringing 360 barley grains together. A brilliant ready-reckoner.

We remembered what we had been told by the expert:

'The barleycorns are more for calculational convenience rather than being considered as actual barleycorns.'

By now we had confidently concluded that this statement was entirely wrong because even modern barley seeds replicate every aspect of the Sumerian/Babylonian weights very accurately.

As previously stated, the use of grains, meaning barley and wheat grains, still exists within the imperial system of measurements. In this case the most rudimentary experiment will prove to anyone that the grains used in the imperial system have, during the passing of centuries, become divorced from genuine wheat or barley seeds. They have essentially become symbols. Experts in this field have doubtless come to believe, or were taught to believe, that the same is true in terms of Sumerian grains or barley seeds. We respectfully suggest that those involved in the study of Sumerian weights and measures disregard, for a while at least, what they have learned and try these experiments for themselves. We are confident they will come to the same conclusions.

The Megalithic Principle and Freemasonry

By Christopher Knight

I joined Freemasonry back in 1976 for the simple reason that I wanted to know what these men where doing behind their closed doors and obscured windows. It did not take too long to realize that even the most senior practitioners had virtually no idea where their weird old rituals came from or what they meant. Between 1989 and 2003 I researched and co-authored four books with fellow Freemason Robert Lomas, starting with *The Hiram Key* which was a first tentative and speculative attempt to make sense of the oddball rituals of the many degrees of Freemasonry.

As our research became more and more focused, Robert and I found ourselves being taken further and further back in time to the Old Testament period and beyond. Here we found that science and religion had once been two sides of the same coin, with the study and worship of the planet Venus being connected with king-making and stone-building. From the Megalithic sites of Britain to the Temple of Jerusalem we found evidence of careful Venus observation that appeared to be associated with birth, death and resurrection.

The entire layout of a masonic temple is astronomical in design, with the three principal officers placed in the east, south and west to mark the rising Sun, noon and the setting Sun. There are two large pillars in the east that represent the freestanding pillars of Boaz and Jachin from the Old Testament that marked the north/south extremes of the solstice sunrises in the original temple, supposedly built for King Solomon.

A candidate for membership is made to represent a worker in stone and in the all-important third degree of Freemasonry he or she is ritually 'killed' and resurrected in near total darkness as the planet Venus symbolically rises in the east ahead of the Sun.

As mentioned in the closing chapter of this book the theme of building in stone being linked to astronomical events is central to these rituals, and God is referred to by Freemasons as 'The Great Architect of the Universe' or 'The Grand Geometrician of the Universe'. This description of the Creator emphasizes the importance of the measurements of both heaven and Earth.

Although this book has nothing directly to do with Freemasonry, I believe that it finally ends my personal quest, for in solving some part of the riddle of the Megalithic Yard, Alan and I have also identified the inspiration that lies behind Freemasonry. Masonic ritual used today states that the real secret of the Order was lost 3,000 years ago and substituted secrets were created until such time as the original ones will be recovered. I believe that time has come.

The picture that I see, built up through researching and writing five books, is that more than 5,000 years ago some unknown group taught the inhabitants of western Europe how to create a measure that was taken directly from Venus, the 'Queen of Heaven'. This divine unit, designated the Megalithic Yard by the man who recovered it, was the cornerstone of civilization. The power of ancient priesthood lay in their knowledge of working with stone, understanding astronomy and the

An 18th-century masonic stamp depicting the central importance of measuring the world and its place in the universe. One pillar carries the Earth and the other the globe of the heavens. The instruments of measurement, the compass and tri-square, surround the letter 'G', signifying God, otherwise known as the 'Grand Geometrician of the Universe'. Above are the Sun and the Moon, surrounded by the planets. In the centre is the 'All-seeing Eye' from which no-one can ever hide.

ability to give their flock measurement!

At some point, probably well before 2000 BC, cultures in the Mediterranean adopted the principles of the geometry used by the Megalithic builders of the British Isles. This knowledge extended from Malta to Crete and the city states of Phoenicia on the coast that we now know as Israel and the Lebanon. The Minoan culture adapted the principles to create their own unit based on this 366 geometry and the Phoenician knowledge passed to another Canaanite group of tribes, later knows as Jews, from the principal tribe of Judah.

Like the British Isles and Brittany, Malta and Israel have Megalithic structures scattered across them and the Old Testament gives detailed evidence of how the Canaanite rituals were adopted for king-making.

In the Jewish state they were also associated with the ritualized slaughter of royal children to ensure God's support for their reign, which apparently was allowed to run for just 40 years. This 40-year period mentioned throughout the Bible was unquestionably linked to the study of the cycle of Venus, which is so reliable that it forms a perfect calendar and clock.

By mechanisms fully described in *The Book of Hiram* the memory of these prehistoric secrets was transmitted by the remnants of the Order of the Knights Templar who took their rituals to Scotland at the beginning of the 14th century when their luck had run out and they were on the run from King Philip of France and Pope Clement V. This was one of the few safe places on the planet because the king of the Scots, Robert the Bruce, had recently been excommunicated from the Church.

As hereditary Grand Master Masons of Scotland, the once dominant St. Clair family had nurtured this ancient knowledge until such time as it was safe to create a new order that we know today as Freemasonry. The opportunity came in 1601 when a Scottish Freemason (James VI of Scotland) became King James I of England, but a little over a century later Freemasonry had to hide itself in London as war had broken out with the Jacobites of Scotland.

In 1715 a Jacobite army marched deep into England and English Freemasons began to walk away from their lodges (meeting places) for fear of being taken as supporters of the enemy. Two years later a small group of London lodges joined forces to try to save the Order from imminent extinction. They did so by forming a new Grand Lodge and by denying all knowledge of where Freemasonry had come from. This mass amnesia worked and Freemasonry began to grow into a major international organization with the United Grand Lodge of England still claiming original authority.

Today, the official line is still, 'We don't know anything before 1717', and hundreds of thousands of men (and women) around the world play out prehistoric rituals in their astronomically-designed temples under the light of the planet Venus, as they say their prayers to the Grand Geometrician of the Universe.

Christians, Jews, Muslims, Hindus and others come together to share substituted secrets connected with the working of stones, the skills of measurement and a shared awe of the workings of the Great Architect of the Universe.

But Freemasonry is dying. Dying at the very moment that we are starting to understand the nature of the original secrets: the units of measurement that truly describe both heaven and Earth.

Index